CL - 3rd ed.

BUSINESS A PROFESSION

Also by LOUIS D. BRANDEIS

In REPRINTS OF ECONOMIC CLASSICS

Other People's Money [1932]

BUSINESS

A PROFESSION

BY

LOUIS D. BRANDEIS

[1914]

REPRINTS OF ECONOMIC CLASSICS

Augustus M. Kelley · Publishers

NEW YORK 1971

First Edition 1914

(Boston: Small, Maynard & Company, 1914)

REPRINTED 1971 BY
AUGUSTUS M. KELLEY · PUBLISHERS
REPRINTS OF ECONOMIC CLASSICS
New York New York 10001

. . . .

ISBN 0-678-00855-8
LCN 68-55491

. . . .

PRINTED IN THE UNITED STATES OF AMERICA
by SENTRY PRESS, NEW YORK, N. Y. 10019

Louis D. Brandeis

PUBLISHERS' NOTE

In response to a demand that there be brought together in one volume the chief public utterances of Mr. Louis D. Brandeis, and because they feel that this demand is the natural outgrowth of Mr. Brandeis's vital interest in matters of large public importance, his success in pointing out the logical outcome of greatly confused conditions, his ability and wisdom in making a sound diagnosis and formulating a hopeful treatment of problems of peculiar difficulty, and his unselfishness and untiring devotion at all times to the common good, the publishers present the papers here compiled, in the belief that they will be of unique interest and of permanent value.

Of the papers here gathered, Mr. Poole's foreword appeared in shorter form in *The American Magazine;* "Business—A Profession," in *System;* "Organized Labor and Efficiency," in *The Survey;* "The Road to Social Efficiency," in *The Outlook;* "Our New Peonage: Discretionary Pensions," in *The Independent;* "The Incorporation of Trades Unions," in *The Green Bag;* "How Boston Solved the Gas Problem," in *The American Review of Reviews;* "Savings Bank Insurance," "Trusts and Efficiency," and "Trusts and the Export Trade," in *Collier's;* "Competition that Kills," in *Harper's Weekly;* "The New Haven —An Unregulated Monopoly," in the *Boston Journal;* "An Aid to Railroad Efficiency," in *The Engineering Magazine;* and "The Opportunity in the Law," in *The American Law Review.* Grateful acknowledgment is made to the editors of these publications for their kind permission to reprint.

CONTENTS

BRANDEIS[1]

A REMARKABLE RECORD OF UNSELFISH WORK DONE
IN THE PUBLIC INTEREST

BY ERNEST POOLE

DURING the Ballinger investigation, in which he was the driving force, he frequently began his day at four o'clock in the morning. His pitiless examinations of witnesses and the startling disclosures he made are widely known. But the man himself is little known, for the man is self-effacing.

He is fifty-seven years old, over medium height, his rugged figure slightly stooped. His face, with its high forehead, prominent cheek bones, deep-set eyes and heavy lines about the broad and sensitive mouth, gives an impression of immense force, of a mind keen, subtle, trained, a mind of large vision, big ideals. And yet it is a likable face; his manner is kindly and he has many devoted friends. His private practice is one of the largest in New England, but more than half his time is spent in public legal work.

[1] Published in the "American Magazine" in February, 1911, and now revised.

And for this work he takes no fees. In an address some years ago he said:

"It is true that at the present time the lawyer does not hold that position with the people which he held fifty years ago; but the reason is in my opinion not lack of opportunity. It is because, instead of holding a position of independence between the wealthy and the people, prepared to curb the excesses of either, the able lawyers have to a great extent allowed themselves to become an adjunct of the great corporations, and have neglected their obligation to use their powers for the protection of the people. If we are to solve the important economic, social and industrial questions which have become political questions also, it seems to me clear that the attitude of the lawyer in this respect must be materially changed. . . . The great opportunity of the American Bar is and will be to stand again as it did in the past, ready to protect also the interests of the people."

Of this work in the people's service, his story is a unique example:

THE ORIGIN OF BRANDEIS

He was born in 1856, in Louisville, Ky. He is a Jew. For a century back his family was made up of men of means, education, social ideals. His maternal grandfather took an active part in Poland's struggle of 1830. His father sympathized deeply with the Bohemian movement of

1848. And in Kentucky, before the war, his father and his uncle were both intense abolitionists. "My earliest memories," he told me, "were of the war. One exceedingly painful memory is of a licking I got in school on the morning after Bull Run. I remember helping my mother carry out food and coffee to the men from the North. The streets seemed full of them always. But there were times when the rebels came so near that we could hear the firing. At one such time my father moved us over the river. Those were my first memories."

Later the family went abroad, and he was placed in a Dresden school. His father suggested that he remain in Europe and take up an academic career. But the son refused. "I was a terrible little individualist in those days," he said, "and the German paternalism got on my nerves. One night, for instance, coming home late and finding I had forgotten my key, I whistled up to awaken my roommate; and for this I was reprimanded by the police. This made me homesick. In Kentucky you could whistle. . . . I wanted to go back to America, and I wanted to study law. My uncle, the abolitionist, was a lawyer; and to me nothing else seemed really worth while."

When the panic of 1873 brought to his father

heavy losses in business, he still held to his course. He entered the Harvard Law School, working his way; he did his eyes an injury from which they have never fully recovered; and at the end of two years the authorities suspended the rules to let him take his degree *at twenty*. "Those years," he said, "were among the happiest of my life. I worked! For me the world's center was Cambridge." This enthusiasm he retained, becoming the organizer, in 1886, of the Harvard Law School Association.

At twenty-two he began practice in Boston. Before he was thirty his practice was large, and since then it has steadily grown. "I had my share of big corporation work," he told me. "I even worked for a trust or two. Perhaps that is one reason why I'm not a corporation lawyer now."

He had many friends in the literary and musical circles of Boston. But his deeper interest was in social economic problems. "As a whole," he said, "I have not got as much from books as I have from tackling concrete problems. I have generally run up against a problem, have painfully tried to think it out, with a measure of success, and have then read a book and found to my surprise that some other chap was before me.

"I first went through the stage of charitable work." He served on his district committee, visiting in person the applicants for relief. In the late eighties he acted as counsel in a movement to reform certain state relief institutions, and early in the nineties he took the lead in a long and thorough investigation into the public charitable institutions of Boston.

When he married in 1891, he had already made up his mind to give more and more time to public work, and with this purpose his wife was in thorough accord. Though his income was large, they agreed from the start upon a most simple scale of living, so leaving time and money free for the series of public struggles in which he has engaged ever since.

In one of his early efforts there is a certain grim humor. In 1897 he went to Washington to appear *for the consumer* in the Dingley Tariff hearing. I quote from a paper of that date: "Mr. Louis D. Brandeis, the brilliant young Bostonian who appeared before the Ways and Means Committee to-day on behalf of the consumers of the United States, did not receive a very cordial welcome. . . . 'I desire,' he said, 'to speak in behalf of those who form a far larger part of the people of this country than any who have found representation here.' . . .

At this point there were signs of restlessness.
Chairman Dingley felt called upon to tell the
gentleman that this was not an appropriate
time for a speech on free trade. A Democratic
member said he supposed it would be in order
for one man to appear for the consumer. Mr.
Brandeis continued, and was again interrupted
by laughter and jeers. But Mr. Dalzell re-
marked, 'Oh, let him run down.'" And so this
lone representative of the consumer was allowed
five minutes more.

HIS FIRST BIG FIGHT FOR THE PUBLIC

But his first important public struggle was
over the traction system in Boston. On the one
side were big financial interests, the political
machine and the press; on the other, a handful
of citizens creating public opinion. Brandeis
was their counsel, and admittedly the brains of
the fight.

For years he had felt that franchises were
public property which should not be given away.
He had seen the situation grow worse. In the
heart of the city the streets available for trolley
lines were few, narrow and crooked, and became
frightfully jammed. To relieve the congestion,
in 1896 the Tremont Street subway was built by
the city. This subway the West End Company,

controlling most of the surface lines, undertook
to lease, and it was over this lease that the first
struggle came. A small group of citizens forced
a hearing. Brandeis appeared as their counsel.
The fight was carried on into the Legislature,
and finally the lease was granted — not for fifty
years, but for twenty years, with a rental to the
city of 4⅞ per cent of the cost of construction.
A victory for the people.

"When I asked Mr. Brandeis for his bill,"
the man at the head of this movement told me,
"I expected to pay a fee of five thousand dollars
at least. 'There is no fee,' he said. 'This is
part of a plan of mine.' And he added that as
soon as he could do so he intended giving the
larger part of his time freely to public work."

The work came soon. In 1897 certain New
York financiers acquired the Boston Elevated
Railway Company. Having bought an old and
impracticable elevated charter, they secured
amendments granting them almost perpetual
rights. They also secured authority to lease
the West End Company's surface lines, and
they asked for a lease of ninety-nine years. Had
this been granted, they would have been in
complete control of the transportation system.
But with a group of vigilant citizens, Brandeis
renewed the contest. The lease was reduced

to twenty-five years, and in other ways the new company's powers were cut down. The company, moreover, had one vulnerable point. The Tremont Street subway, the only connecting link between the two parts of the elevated system, was still under strong municipal control.

Accordingly, when to meet the increasing traffic another subway was asked for in 1900, the company tried to secure the right to build it and own it practically in perpetuity, and also to secure an extension on their Tremont Street subway lease for another twenty years. Over this key to the situation came the main struggle. And here again on the side of the people Brandeis took the lead. When the Public Franchise League was formed, he became its counsel. He was active in winning over the Associated Board of Trade, and in its name a bill which he drafted was introduced providing for the construction of the new subway by the city, with a lease on the same terms as the old one. In support of this bill he appeared at all hearings. He went in person repeatedly to the editors of the hostile press. "It was here," he told me, "that we had our first lessons in making public opinion." Slowly the public sentiment grew. And finally, after a bitter three years' contest, an act almost identical with his original bill was

passed, providing for the construction of one
or more subways by the city, to be leased for a
term not exceeding twenty-five years, at a rental
of $4\frac{1}{2}$ per cent of the cost.

In 1911 the contest over the subway leases
broke out anew. With a "strap-hanging" public clamoring for new subways, the Elevated
Company announced that it could assume no
further burdens without assured possession of
both the new and the old subways and tunnels
for about fifty years. The Railroad and Transit
Commissions indorsed this position, and many
timid citizens, eager for relief from congestion,
were ready to yield. The Public Franchise
League, however, with Brandeis once more leading the fight, opposed this attempt to fasten the
company's grip upon the city, and argued that
the best guarantee such a company can have is
the good will of the public induced by its own
good behavior. This view was speedily cham-
pioned by the press, and an act, drawn under
the guidance of Mr. Brandeis, with the approval of Governor Foss, was finally passed by
the Legislature and accepted by the company,
which provided for the new subways and for
leases subject to termination by either the
city or the company at the end of twenty-five
years.

"Boston has thus established," he writes, "the policy of retaining control of its transportation system. The city will own all the subways, and through this ownership and the right to revoke surface locations, will control the entire traction system, with power to compel corporations to pay what may seem from time to time adequate compensation for the use of the streets."

A STRUGGLE FOR CHEAPER GAS

The next struggle, to secure cheaper gas for Boston, was won in its crisis, not by fighting the company, but by working with it. And for this change of policy Brandeis was responsible.

For twenty years the city's gas companies had been involved in endless scandals. The service was poor and the price was high, one dollar a thousand feet. But all Massachusetts gas companies are subject to strict state control; and, when in 1903 the Boston companies applied for leave to consolidate, the Public Franchise League saw its opportunity. A long and strenuous contest took place over the issue of capital, the Franchise League contending that, if the company were allowed the high capitalization it asked for, lower prices of gas in future would be made impossible. When things had come to a crisis, Brandeis proposed his plan of co-operation. It startled many in the League; some even withdrew, accusing him of being in secret alliance with the trust. But he held to his course, and after earnest discussion the plan was finally carried out. Its main provisions were these:

The company's capital was fixed practically at the limit set by the League at the start. Ninety cents per thousand feet was made the "standard price" of gas. And a "standard dividend" was fixed at seven per cent. This meant a return of less than 4½ per cent on the physical value of the property and on its cost to the present owners. *But the act further provided that for every five-cent reduction in the price of gas, the dividend might be increased one per cent.*

This gave a strong incentive to concentrate all the energy, formerly used in financial and political intrigue, on the making of gas at the lowest possible cost. As a result, the price has been reduced to eighty cents. From 1905 to 1913, $6,247,923.35 in the aggregate has been saved to the consumers, and yet dividends have been increased some two per cent.

"It has been proved," he says, "that a public-service corporation may be managed with

political honesty and yet successfully. To reduce the price of gas we need not only honesty
but also skill, energy and initiative. And this
may be best secured by following those lines of
intelligent self-interest upon which the remarkable industrial advance of America has proceeded. Those who manage our public-service
corporations should be permitted, subject to
proper safeguards, to conduct the enterprise
under the conditions which in ordinary business have proved a sufficient incentive to attract
men of large ability and to insure from them
their utmost efforts for its advancement."

THE NEW HAVEN RAILROAD

Brandeis has led one other fight in New England against a big corporation.

Before 1906 the New York, New Haven &
Hartford Railroad had been steadily gaining
control of transportation in New England.
Among other things it had acquired about
five hundred miles of trolley lines in Massachusetts contrary to the law of the state. And
in 1906 the governor warned the legislature
of the New Haven's encroaching power, urging
legislation to prevent it. The New Haven company contended that having a Connecticut
charter it was not subject to Massachusetts laws.

It invited the state's attorney general to test the validity of this claim, and agreed pending a decision to make no further acquisitions in the state. On this understanding the legislature adjourned without taking action and the attorney general began proceedings. While these were pending, however, the New Haven company, regardless of its promise, acquired more than one-third of the stock of the Boston & Maine Railroad. The legislature then passed an act restraining the New Haven, until July, 1908, from acquiring additional stock in the Boston & Maine or from voting on that already acquired.

Meanwhile public feeling rose high. The Anti-Merger League was formed, with Brandeis for its counsel. The support of thousands of Massachusetts merchants and of commercial and civic organizations and labor unions was secured. Their campaign was pushed with energy, Brandeis engaging in a long series of public debates with the New Haven's vice-president. The railroad, too, had strong support. People were sick of the Boston & Maine's poor service; they believed its management unprogressive and its financial condition weak, and that if the New Haven could gain control it would bring up the service. The danger of monopoly they proposed to remove by legislative control.

Brandeis, however, contended that the Boston & Maine was recovering from its financial weakness and could soon provide needed improvements, but that the New Haven had by its recent excessive expansion become perilously weak, and that the burdens thus assumed must not only prevent its making large improvements, but would create a heavy charge upon all future traffic. Moreover, he cited the scores of railroads, trolley and steamship lines which it had already acquired, and claimed that if the Boston & Maine be added to these, the result must be a monopoly of all transportation by land or water within New England and also between New England and the rest of the country. To control a monopoly so enormous, he declared, would be impossible. One small group of New York financiers would govern absolutely New England's future growth.

Meanwhile the New Haven had presented a bill legalizing the purchase of its Boston & Maine stock. This bill was defeated. In the same year the state Supreme Court, in the case brought by the attorney general, decided that the New Haven was subject to Massachusetts laws and that in acquiring Boston & Maine stock it had

violated the statute. Shortly after this, with
the approval of President Roosevelt, Attorney
General Bonaparte began suit against the New
Haven under the Sherman act. The opponents
of the merger therefore ceased their work, believing that their fight was won.

But in 1909 in Washington a new administration came into power; and in Massachusetts
a new governor was elected, who was favorable
to the New Haven. Late in the session this
governor sent in a special message paving the
way for a bill which empowered the New Haven
to acquire through a holding company all the
stock of the Boston & Maine. Tremendous
pressure was brought to bear, and the bill was
passed. "The passage of this bill," said French,
the federal district attorney, "does not change
matters in the slightest degree regarding the
federal government's merger suits against the
New Haven road." But four days later, on the
same day that French was pressing the court
to set down the case for argument, Attorney
General Wickersham ordered the suit dropped.

With all legal obstacles thus removed, the
holding company was formed, and by this means
the control of New England's transportation
was delivered to the New Haven.

Brandeis predicted an increase in rates if the

merger were allowed. Taking the two roads'
own estimates, their passenger rates were soon
increased by about $1,500,000 a year, and they
applied for increases in freight rates which exceeded $2,000,000 more. "The need for more
revenue was caused," Brandeis maintained,
"not so much by increase in operating expenses
as by the financial burdens assumed in their
sudden excessive expansion, purchasing properties at high values, borrowing money at high
rates."

In no controversy in which he has engaged
has his judgment been so emphatically and
dramatically vindicated as here. Month by
month the operation of what he calls the "in-
exorable law of arithmetic" made itself felt —
until railroad service in New England, especially
upon the Boston & Maine, became intolerable. Frightful accidents took place. And
complaints multiplied to such an extent that
the Interstate Commerce Commission finally
ordered a thorough investigation of the whole
situation. The results of this investigation and
Commissioner Prouty's report are now well
known. The criticisms of the New Haven's
financial policy made by Brandeis six years before were more than sustained; and at the present time the Department of Justice in Wash-

ington and the Governor of Massachusetts are trying to undo the work of their predecessors in office, break the New England transportation monopoly and restore sane and healthy conditions.

A BRILLIANT SUCCESS

Meanwhile Mr. Brandeis had undertaken a project which has since met with brilliant success.

In 1905, in the investigation into the Equitable Life Assurance Society, as unpaid counsel for the protective committee of policy holders, he drafted recommendations urging radical changes to reduce the enormous waste of the system and provide safeguards against abuse. It is said that Grover Cleveland, one of the newly appointed trustees, gave these recommendations to Paul Morton, the incoming president of the Equitable, and told him that on these principles the reorganization should proceed. They are, in the main, the same principles later insisted upon by Charles E. Hughes and embodied in the Armstrong bill.

This work led Brandeis to a close study of the insurance business. The total amount of insurance in the ninety leading companies he found to be nearly thirteen billions of dollars, more in amount than the value of all the railroads in the country at that time, their total income exceeding the revenues of the federal government. Nearly half the total assets were in the hands of three Wall Street companies; and this vast accumulation of quick capital gave them an ever-tightening grip on the business of the country. "The economic menace of past ages," he said in an address at that time, "was the *dead hand*, which gradually acquired a large part of all available lands. The greatest economic menace of to-day is a very *live* hand, these great insurance companies which control so large a part of our quick capital."

On the one hand a prodigious concentration of money power; on the other, an intimate concern of every man. In the ninety companies there were outstanding over 21,000,000 policies affecting directly or indirectly about 30,000,000 men, women and children. And through the waste and abuses inherent in the system the cost of insurance was terribly high. This was doubly true of "industrial insurance," purchased mainly by the poor, the policies being for small amounts and the premiums collected weekly from house to house. Mainly through this extravagant method, about two-fifths of the policy-holders' money went into running expenses.

Brandeis undertook to work out some plan
by which the wage-earners of the country might
get cheaper insurance, and by which in the
course of time the business might be taken out
of the hands of a few and placed in social institutions all over the land. In Massachusetts
such institutions already existed. There were
in that state 189 savings banks, managed by
about three thousand men who regarded them
as quasi-public trusts and so gave their services.
The cost of management was less than one-tenth
of that in insurance companies. Why not add
insurance departments to these banks? He drew
up a tentative plan, for months he lectured and
wrote on the subject, the Savings Bank Insurance
League was formed, and a bill which he drafted
was introduced, empowering savings banks of
the state to establish insurance departments.

This bill was bitterly opposed by the old industrial companies. But the League was hard
at work. Volunteer speakers stumped the
entire state; for six months Brandeis spoke
from two to six nights every week; a petition
of 150,000 names was presented, and tens of
thousands of letters poured in on the legislature. In 1907 the bill passed. And by the
end of 1908, in two banks the system was
established.

From their earnings, after paying all charges and setting aside all possible reserves, they declared at the end of the first year an 8⅓ per cent dividend to the policy holders—a sum equal to one month's premium. And besides, the policy holders got a rate twenty-two per cent less than that given by the old industrial companies.

Since then two more banks have adopted the system, and their reports in January, 1914, showed more than eight thousand policies in force, representing more than $3,000,000 of insurance. A fifth-year dividend has been declared on the monthly premium policies, equalling twenty per cent of a year's premiums.

This reduction has resulted from radical changes. In place of the old wasteful method of house-to-house solicitation, the League began a campaign of insurance education. Volunteer speakers, together with paid insurance instructors, spoke in factory towns, and the manufacturers gave cordial support. Through their aid meetings were held, literature was distributed, and finally the instructor went through the factory talking in person to each employee. In this way the business has been secured with little expense. And the old method of house-to-house collection has been also done away with. Premiums are paid either through the employer or at the bank.

Two hundred employers of labor throughout the state are now co-operating with the banks and with the state by becoming unpaid agencies for the receipt of applications and the transmission of premiums of their employees.

Far more significant than the success of these banks has been the effect on the old industrial companies. There is space here for but one of the concessions made. For more than twenty years they had made no reduction in premiums; but since the new movement started their premiums have been reduced on an average of about twenty per cent. This means a saving to Massachusetts wage-earners of over $1,000,000 a year, and to the people of the country it will probably mean within a few years an annual saving of from fifteen to twenty millions.

"Our work so far," said Brandeis, "has affected only industrial insurance, but I believe that workingmen's insurance in America is soon to assume gigantic proportions and become the bulk of all insurance. Shall these wage-earners be served by an exploiting business, with dangerous power in a few hands, or by public and quasi-public institutions all over the country?"

SHORTER HOURS FOR WOMEN WORKERS

In other big struggles affecting wage-earners, Brandeis has taken a leading part. One was in behalf of our millions of women factory workers.

In 1907, in Oregon, a law restricting women's work in factories and laundries to ten hours in one day was contested and carried to the United States Supreme Court. And through the National Consumers' League, Brandeis undertook its defence.

The law had been attacked as against the constitutional right of freedom of contract. This freedom, however, is subject to the police powers of the states. If it could be proved that the legislature in passing the law had reasonable grounds for believing that a day longer than ten hours is so injurious to women as to be a danger to the community, the court must hold the law constitutional.

Brandeis saw that the crux of the case lay in the human facts involved. He accordingly outlined a brief and called upon the Consumers' League to collect and arrange the facts. Miss Josephine Goldmark of the League undertook the work. All available evidence was collected. With this he went before the court, and the result was a unanimous decision upholding the law.

But he saw that the fight was not over, and he determined to strengthen the evidence. Under his guidance Miss Goldmark again set to work, with a large corps of assistants, to prepare an exhaustive brief on the subject. It was ready none too soon. In 1909, in Illinois, a similar law was contested before the Supreme Court of the state, and again Brandeis led the defence. The manufacturer's claim, that a certain woman thirty-five years in his employ could not earn a living wage unless she worked over ten hours a day, acted as a boomerang. And the result was again a victory.

In 1911 Brandeis was invited by the attorney general of Ohio to assist in the defence of a somewhat similar Ohio statute regulating hours for women. He submitted a brief in this case before the Supreme Court of the state, which held the law constitutional. The case was carried on appeal to the Supreme Court of the United States. Brandeis again filed a brief and took part in the oral argument. And the Supreme Court, in 1914, upheld the law. In 1912 he was again active in the defence of the Illinois law, which was again the subject of attack, its scope having been widely extended.

In November, 1913, a request for assistance came from a new source. This was in regard to the minimum wage rulings of the Oregon Industrial Welfare Commission. The commission was established by statute in 1913 and empowered to establish such wages, hours of labor and conditions of work as appeared, after investigation, to be necessary for preservation of the health and welfare of the employees. The minimum wages for women employed in factories and stores were promulgated by the commission in September, 1913. Constitutionality of the act under which these orders were issued was contested in the courts, and at the commission's request Brandeis again, with Miss Goldmark's aid, filed a brief showing the relation of wages to health, morals and efficiency. In March, 1914, a unanimous decision was handed down sustaining the law.

In his work in these labor cases there are two points of especial significance.

First, the method of argument marks a revolutionary change. Hitherto such cases had been argued *deductively*, from the legal precedents, upon abstract theories of what is right and what is wrong. But the method used here is *inductive*. The first Illinois brief contains only four pages of strictly legal argument; the remaining

605 pages go straight to the medical, social and economic facts involved. And the spirit of modern science thus successfully brought into court will doubtless have a far-reaching effect on future court decisions.

Second, the brief is significant for what it proves *beyond* its point. For the knowledge of the whole civilized world on the subject of overwork is assembled here. It is shown that in this tense machine age an hour's work means far more than it did a century back; that excessive work not only weakens the body and opens the way to diseases, but itself produces an actual poison, "the toxin of fatigue"; that fatigue weakens self-control and leads to the use of drink and drugs; that overwork tends to exhaust the central nervous system upon which the vital functions depend; and finally that through overwork the danger of accidents is increased, the greatest number of accidents coming between eleven and twelve in the morning and between four and six in the afternoon, when the senses are dulled by fatigue.

Overwork is especially fatal to women. By a terrific array of evidence it is shown that working women are sick far more often than men, that their mortality is higher, and that in thousands of cases the child-bearing function is

impaired. Sterility, miscarriage, stillbirth —
each is common; and children born to exhausted
women are at birth below normal weight and
size. Through the mother's weakness and her
absence from her baby, the infant death rate
is terribly high, while thousands grow up weak-
lings. And the danger is not to health alone.
For a mother returning exhausted at night, with
the cooking and washing still to be done, has
little will or energy left; and the moral hold of
the home is lost. The very preservation of a
people, therefore, is threatened by such overwork. In districts where it has long existed
actual race degeneration has set in.

The evidence shows, on the other hand, that
shorter hours have resulted in vastly improving
the whole tone of the community; that they
have worked no injury to the employer, for by
the increased efficiency as much work was done
as before, generally more; and that, instead of
lowering wages, with the resulting increase of
output wages also have increased.

In the face of such evidence it becomes plain
that a ten-hour law hardly touches this intricate
problem. Hours of labor both for women and
men will undoubtedly be still further shortened.
And as a sound scientific basis for future legislation, this brief has been still further expanded.

"In every public job that Brandeis has tackled," said one of his friends, "you will find this same long-headed view. Out of the thick of each fight he is in, he seems to look into the future."

A GREAT TASK ACHIEVED

This is true of his work in settling strikes.

The cloakmakers' strike in New York, in the summer of 1910, involved some seventy thousand employees and a business of $180,000,000 a year. Conditions were bad. The hours were long and irregular, and through a system of subcontracting the pay for most workers was wretchedly low. The strike was bitter, sudden, chaotic; men starved on $1.50 a week, and refused to hear of compromise. The dispute had centred around the "closed shop." The union would listen to no terms without it; employers were equally set against it; two attempts at conference had split upon this rock.

Then Brandeis was called in. It was midsummer, his time for vacation; but he came at once to New York, as usual giving his services. He soon won the confidence of both sides.

"He was a man," said the union's socialist lawyer, "to whom we did not hesitate to talk openly from the start. He showed a broad mind and a fine sense of fairness. It was the most wonderful handling of a strike situation that I've ever seen."

This is shown by the minutes of the conference. For the class struggle was here deep, fundamental, made bitter by the chaos of the past. Repeatedly the two sides clashed. But repeatedly, with sound reasoning and demand for the facts, the arbitrator came between. Knowing the closed-shop issue to be the danger-point, he persistently put it off, in order that first both sides might see that on all other points they could agree. When it came up at last he offered a compromise plan (his invention) "the preferential union shop." This was refused, and the strike went on. But a month later an agreement was reached. Wages were raised, hours reduced, the system of subcontracting abolished, and many other improvements made. But by far the most important result was the adoption, in a more definite form, of the Brandeis plan for a preferential union shop. The final agreement describes it as follows:

"A shop where union standards as to working conditions, hours of labor and rates of wages prevail, and where, when hiring help, union men are preferred; it being recognized that since there are differences in degree of skill

among those employed in the trade, employers
shall have freedom of selection as between one
union man and another, and shall not be confined to any list nor bound to follow any prescribed order whatever. . . . The Manufacturers' Association, however, declare their belief
in the union, and that all who desire its benefits
should share in its burdens."

To make it effective, provisions were added
for a price committee, a shop chairman, a committee on grievances, a board of sanitary control and a board of arbitration. On this board,
Brandeis was chosen as the third man.

During the three years since then, the development of the industry has completely justified
his anticipations. There has been no general
strike. The rate of wages, increased in 1910,
has been maintained, and concerns which for
some time paid below the union scale have been
compelled to conform to it. In August, 1913,
a demand having been made for higher wages
and the matter referred to the Board of Arbitration, the board caused an intensive study
of the whole subject to be made, the report of
which will soon appear. The industry has been
more and more stabilized. The forty-eight-hour
week has been more strictly adhered to, over-
time has been paid double and there has been

an enormous improvement in the sanitary conditions of the shop, a continual raising of the
standards of health. The machinery of the
Protocol, or working agreement, has been
enormously facilitated and improved. A body
of industrial laws and precedents has grown up
based on justice to both sides. Of eight thousand
cases arising in two years, only nine had to be
referred finally to the Board of Arbitration, the
others having been settled by the parties themselves. Of course there has been agitation and
misunderstanding; but, where such excitement
formerly would have led to disastrous strikes, it
now passes harmlessly over the industry. The
Board of Arbitration has become a supreme
industrial court to which great problems of
fundamental policy alone have been referred.
A better spirit has prevailed between the two
parties, a spirit of conciliation. The leaders on
both sides have been educated to the standpoint which Brandeis had originally taken, that
of considering the industry as a whole. It is
still an experiment, imperfect and full of the
difficulties inherent in industrial relations. It
demands the greatest possible self-control on
both sides. But it contains the germ of a great
idea; an element of industrial statesmanship.

"Prolonged peace and prosperity," Brandeis

maintains, "can rest only on the foundation of industrial liberty. Industrial democracy should ultimately attend political democracy. Industrial absolutism is not merely impossible in this country at the present time, but is most undesirable. Our employers can no more afford to be absolute masters of their employees than they can afford to submit to the mastery of their employees. Bluff and bluster have no place here. The spirit must be 'Come, let us reason together.' Such conferences are necessarily time-consuming, but the time cannot be better spent. There are no short cuts to evolution."

THE LAWYER IN THE BALLINGER CASE

Until his appearance before the Interstate Commerce Commission as counsel for shippers in the Freight Rate Advance Case, the most widely known of all his work in the people's service was done in the Ballinger investigation.

About two weeks before the investigation began, he became counsel for Glavis. Those two weeks he spent delving into the mass of details involved. It was an amazing instance of swift absorption. The committee, it was feared, would make short work of Glavis; but if this were intended, it was made impossible by the brilliant history of the whole matter which Brandeis gave at the start.

His task was hard; for the whole administration was set against the investigation. To the requests for records there were delays, and later even denials. But over what records he could secure, he used to work in his room late at night, and he was often at work again at four o'clock in the morning. Out of these dry records he tried to build up the part each man had played, to visualize the story. And out of this patient searching came two disclosures which startled the country.

For their understanding a few dates are needed. On August 18, 1909, Glavis submitted his charges. On September 6 Ballinger submitted a mass of documents in reply. On September 13 the President exonerated Ballinger and dismissed Glavis. Two months later Glavis appealed to the country. On December 21. the Senate requested the President to transmit to Congress *any reports, statements, papers or documents upon which he had relied in reaching his conclusion.* And the President complied. Among the papers submitted were a summary and a report by Attorney General Wickersham, dated September 11.

In the course of time Brandeis began to sus-
pect that these Wickersham papers had not
been written on September 11. If so, why had
not the President referred to them in his letter
of September 13? Moreover, they were dated
only five days after Ballinger had submitted
his mass of evidence. How could the Attorney
General have made in five days so careful an
analysis of the huge mass of confused and intricate papers submitted, *so unfair* an analysis,
adroitly keeping back some facts and giving undue weight to others? Finally he found definite
proof. The report referred to a certain statute
as mentioned by Glavis in his letter. Glavis
had *not* mentioned it in his letter to the President. But he *had* mentioned it in his Collier's
article *over two months later*.

Still Brandeis hesitated. The officials involved were so high. If he failed to completely
prove his point, the recoil would be terrific.
But when Finney, a subordinate to Wickersham,
was on the stand, Brandeis asked him such
questions as these: "What do you know of that
report? *When did you first see it? When did
you first hear of it?*" And though Finney's
answers were evasive, from the startled expression on his face and on certain other faces,
Brandeis finally made up his mind. He put

the question that afternoon. Had not the Attorney General antedated his report?

"The silence in that room," said one, "was instant, terribly intense. For everyone knew that before risking such a question, Brandeis must have proof of his facts." Finney evaded the question. Two days later Brandeis called for a statement from Wickersham. The committee refused to make the request. But a resolution making a like request was introduced into Congress, and in a communication to the Committee of the House the Attorney General admitted that his report was not written until long after the day of its date, long after the President's decision. A similar admission was made later by the President.

At the time of this admission Ballinger was on the stand. Brandeis had long been insisting that this chief witness be called. He knew the risk he ran of turning the public against him if he pressed his man too hard; but he took the risk. "I have never heard," said one lawyer, "so relentless an examination. When any other man would have stopped out of sheer pity, still he kept on." But the bursts of rage from the witness, his misstatements and self-contradictions, had a fatally damaging effect. Repeatedly he made denials, which a series of keen, quiet questions broke down. These questions showed a disturbingly accurate knowledge of Ballinger's every move from August 26 to September 13, his itinerary in minutest detail, down to the trains he took, exact hours of arrival, who met him at stations, where they went. At one point Senator Root intervened. "Mr. Brandeis," he asked indignantly, "were you having this man followed by a detective?" Brandeis smiled and answered, "No."

"As a matter of fact," as he later told the committee, "this wonderful detective work was quite simply done. I knew Ballinger's main itinerary. I then secured back copies of the local newspapers in the places he visited; and in them, quite naturally, I acquired my marvellous knowledge."

When Wickersham had made his admission, Brandeis began pressing Ballinger upon another matter. He knew that Ballinger's subordinate, Lawler, had drafted a letter on which the President had largely based his letter of exoneration. This Lawler letter had never been mentioned. Brandeis knew of it from Kerby, Lawler's stenographer, who had refused to come out with a statement. He now questioned Ballinger on the same subject. And it was when the latter showed by his answers his resolve to keep back the truth that Kerby decided to state what he knew. Further, he said he had found the note-book in which he had taken Lawler's dictation, and had had photographs made of the pages containing the letter. Here at last was definite proof.

Close on the Ballinger denial, the Kerby statement appeared in a Western paper. The telegraphic report, which reached the White House at noon, failed to include the fact that Kerby had proof. The White House issued a denial. Later in the day the full report, in-cluding the proof, appeared in a Washington paper. The next day the President sent to the Investigating Committee a long statement ad-mitting the truth of what Kerby had said. The President stated among other things that he had asked Mr. Lawler "to prepare an opinion as if he were President."

From these two exposures it was plain that the President, in response to the Senate's re-quest, had sent to Congress an important paper on which he had *not* relied in reaching his con-clusions, because it was not in existence; and also that he had *omitted* to send another import-ant paper on which he *did* rely, from which he *copied portions*. These disclosures did much to convince the public. For if the administration must so shield a man, how unfit must he be to continue in office!

Of the work of Brandeis here, the most interesting part to me is his handling of the reporters. From the start, knowing how little he had to hope for from the majority of the committee, he presented his case direct to the American people. Night after night in his room he worked with the newspaper men, explaining the day's significant points. And the result of this work was great. For Mr. Ballinger's resignation was mainly due to the strong public sentiment made through the press.

In his closing argument, Brandeis stated what he believed to be the real significance of the work. "This investigation," he said, "has been referred to as a struggle for conservation, a struggle against the special interests. It is that: but it is far more. In its essence, it is the struggle for democracy, the struggle of the small man against the overpowering influence of the big; politically as well as financially, the struggle to establish the right of every American to equal justice in the public service as well as in the courts, that no official is so highly stationed that he may trample ruthlessly and unjustly upon even the humblest American citizen. The cause of Glavis is the cause of the common people, and more especially the cause of the hundreds of thousands of government officials."

Not long after this, Brandeis entered a contest of greater magnitude than any in which he had ever before engaged. He became counsel for all the trade organizations of the Atlantic seaboard in the hearing on the proposed advance in railroad rates before the Interstate Commerce Commission.

"I opposed these rates," he told me, "both because the method of raising them, by horizontal, arbitrary and undiscriminating increase, was a departure from all previous practice in rate making, disregarding the effect of the increase upon the business affected; and also on the ground that marry of the railroads, if they needed additional income at all, needed it because of a reckless policy of aggrandizement and other financial excesses.

"But the point that struck me most was this: While the railroads were seeking to increase rates in order to overcome the increase of operating cost, largely due to increased wages which would amount to a small per cent, there were immense possibilities of introducing economies of many times the amount. For the railroads, during the last ten years, through the practical elimination of competition and through their increase beyond the unit of greatest efficiency, had come to be even less economically operated than before. The main economies of operation they had made were those resulting from the levelling of grades, elimination of curves, introduction of larger cars and engines — in short, improvement in plant. They had left practically unworked the field of attaining *greater efficiency through the new science of management* — a science which in other industries was already being developed with wonderful results, a science by which the efficiency of the individual workman was often more than doubled, resulting in both largely increased compensation to the worker and increased profit to the employer.

"I therefore urged that if the roads needed greater income they should resort to increase of managerial efficiency, and that it would but put a premium on uneconomical management to permit an increase of rates simply because there appeared to be need of greater income. This policy was particularly dangerous because of the open declaration of the railroad presidents that the increases sought were but the beginnings of demands for still higher rates, and that the community must accustom itself to the idea that rates generally would continue to increase."

The outcome of this controversy is well known. The commission refused to allow the increase in both the eastern and the western divisions of the railroads of the country. Mr. Brandeis's activity not only had the effect of concentrating public attention upon the case and the real issues involved, but also of creating widespread and unusal interest in the question of scientific management. As one of the engineers said: "By a single stroke Brandeis created a greater advance in scientific management than would otherwise have come in the next quarter of a century."

"The great fact to remember is this," he told me. "The coming *science of management*, in this century, marks an advance comparable only to that made by the coming of the *machine* in the last. The profits from the machine were absorbed by capital. But we have developed a social sense. And now of the profits that are to come from the new scientific management, the people are to have their share. These profits are to be immense. On our railroads alone at least a million dollars a day might be saved by this kind of management. Not all the material resources in our land can compare to this prodigious field, the possibilities of the science which will increase the efficiency of man. And *this* public domain must not be preëmpted."

What the commission thought of Mr. Brandeis's work in this case is indicated by the fact that in the summer of 1913 they engaged him as counsel for the commission itself in the matter of the renewed application of the railroads for a similar general increase in rates, the case which is now going on in Washington.

BRANDEIS AND THE " MONEY TRUST "

His most recent work, at the time of this writing, has been his attack on the "money trust," a work which has had a large share in bringing forward important bills which deal with the trusts of the country.

"On nothing has he ever worked harder," writes Mr. Norman Hapgood, "than on his diagnosis of the money trust, and when his life comes to be written (I hope many years hence) this will be ranked with his railroad work for its effect in accelerating industrial changes. It is indeed more than a coincidence that so many of the things he has been contending for have come to pass. It is seldom that one man puts one idea, not to say many ideas, effectively before the world, but it is no exaggeration to say that Mr. Brandeis is responsible for the now widespread recognition of the inherent weakness of great size. He was the first person who set forth effectively the doctrine that there is a limit to the size of greatest efficiency, and the successful demonstration of that truth is a profound contribution to the subject of trusts. The demonstration is powerfully put in his testimony before the Senate Committee in 1911. In destroying the delusion that efficiency was a common incident of size, he emphasized the possibility of efficiency through intensive development of the individual, thus connecting this principle with his whole study of efficiency, and pointing the way to industrial democracy."

Such, in brief, is the public work of this man in a little over twenty years. For such work he has urged the importance of big successful lawyers keeping themselves free. He has kept himself free: striving to hold a position of absolute independence "between the wealthy and the people." On the one hand, he has no close political ties: he has declined every proffer of office, has occasionally even refused to work for or against any candidate. On the other, he has no connection with any big corporation. "I would rather have clients," he told me, "than

be somebody's lawyer." He has steadily tried
to rid himself of all property influence; he has
no investments in the Boston public utilities,
and made it a rule not to take a financial interest in a business for which he was counsel. His
income is large, but he spends little. He is a
generous giver. "I have only one life, and it's
short enough," he said. "Why waste it on
things that I don't want most? And I don't
want money or property most. I want to be
free."

In his home, the standard set about twenty
years back has remained the same. He lives in
a simple house and he has few material wants —
keeping himself free from the encumbrance of
things. In his house you at once feel at home.
He has many warm friends and a wide acquaint-
ance; he is a keen appreciator of men. "It's
hard to interview Brandeis," said a well-known
writer. "He wastes your time interviewing
you."

Each year more of his time is given freely to
public work. Each year certain big special
interests grow more bitter against him, for he
is a patient, pitiless antagonist, and the reforms
he proposes go deep.

"We are sure to have for the next generation
an ever-increasing contest between those who

have and those who have not. There are vital
economic, social and industrial problems to be
solved. And for these we need our ablest men.
The reason why we have not made more progress
in social matters is that these problems have
not been tackled by the practical men of high
ability, like those who have worked on industrial
inventions and enterprises. We need *social inventions*,
each of many able men adding his
work until the invention is perfected.

"I have no rigid social philosophy. I have
been too intense on concrete problems of practical justice.
And yet I can see that the tendency
is steadily toward governmental control. The
government must keep order *not only physically
but socially*. In old times the law was meant to
protect each citizen from oppression by physical
force. But we have passed to a subtler civilization;
from oppression by force we have come
to oppression in other ways. And the law must
still protect a man from the things that rob him
of his freedom, whether the oppressing force
be physical or of a subtler kind.

"There is no such thing as freedom for a man
who under normal conditions is not financially
free. We must therefore find means to create
in the individual financial independence against
sickness, accidents, unemployment, old age and

the dread of leaving his family destitute, if he suffer premature death. For we have become practically a world of employees; and, if a man is to have real freedom of contract in dealing with his employer, he must be financially independent of these ordinary contingencies. Unless we protect him from this oppression, it is foolish to call him free. Moreover, since most men are employees and since men must work to live, the law should see that they are protected from oppression in their work, from excessive hours of labor and other conditions injurious not only to them alone but through them to the common good.

"This principle applies in general to the whole question of property rights. Property must be subject to that control of property which is essential to the enjoyment by every man of a free individual life. And when property is used to interfere with that fundamental freedom of life for which property is *only a means*, then property must be controlled. This applies to the regulation of trusts and railroads, public utilities and all the big industries that control the necessities of life. Laws regulating them, far from being infringements on liberty, are in reality protections against infringements on liberty.

"Property is only a means. It has been a frequent error of our courts that they have made the means an end. Once correct that error, put property back into its right place, and the whole social-legal conception becomes at once consistent. I see no need to amend our Constitution. It has not lost its capacity for expansion to meet new conditions, unless it be interpreted by rigid minds which have no such capacity. Instead of amending the Constitution, I would amend men's economic and social ideals. I believe that our judges are as honest as you can make men. But like all the rest of us they are subject to their environment. And law has always been a narrowing, conservatizing profession. In England it was always easy for a Tory government to find great lawyers for judicial office, but for a Liberal government it was hard. And so it has been throughout history. Nearly all of England's great lawyers were Tories.

"What we must do in America is not to attack our judges, but to educate them. All judges should be made to feel, as many judges already do, that the things needed to protect liberty are radically different from what they were fifty years back. In some courts the judges' conceptions of their own powers must also change. Some judges have decided a law unconstitu-

tional simply because they considered the law
unwise. These judges should be made to feel
that they have no such right, that their business is not to decide whether the view taken by
the legislature is a wise view, but whether a
body of men could reasonably hold such a view.
In the past the courts have reached their con-
clusions largely deductively from preconceived
notions and precedents. The method I have
tried to employ in arguing cases before them has
been inductive, reasoning from the facts.

"In general, I believe that the courts and the
people have been too far apart. There is no
subject so complex that the people cannot be
interested in it and made to see the truth about
it if pains enough be taken; and I believe that a
common agreement of public sentiment should
influence the court's decision on many a question.

"For the aspirations of the people must have
adequate legal expression. Otherwise we shall
have a revolt. The whole industrial world is in
a state of ferment. It is in the main peaceful,
and to a considerable extent silent; but there
is felt to-day very widely the inconsistency in
this condition of political democracy and industrial absolutism. The people are beginning
to doubt whether in the long run democracy and
absolutism can coexist in the same community;

beginning to doubt whether there is really a justification for the great inequalities in the distribution of wealth. This movement must necessarily progress; the people's thought will take shape in action. And it lies with our lawyers to say in what lines that action shall be expressed: wisely and temperately or wildly and intemperately; in lines of evolution or in lines of revolution.

"Young men who feel drawn to the legal profession may rest assured that they will find in it an opportunity for usefulness which is probably unequalled elsewhere. There is and there will be a call upon the legal profession to do a great work for this country."

He is fond of quoting these lines from Euripides, written over two thousand years back, but which have a pregnant meaning for us now:

> Thou hast heard men scorn thy city, call her wild
> Of counsel, mad; thou hast seen the fire of morn
> Flash from her eyes in answer to their scorn!
> Come toil on toil, 't is this that makes her grand,
> Peril on peril! And common states that stand
> In caution, twilight cities, dimly wise —
> Ye know them, for no light is in their eyes!
> *Go forth, my son, and help!*

BUSINESS—A PROFESSION

BUSINESS—A PROFESSION[1]

EACH commencement season we are told by the college reports the number of graduates who have selected the professions as their occupations and the number of those who will enter business. The time has come for abandoning such a classification. Business should be, and to some extent already is, one of the professions. The once meagre list of the learned professions is being constantly enlarged. Engineering in its many branches already takes rank beside law, medicine and theology. Forestry and scientific agriculture are securing places of honor. The new professions of manufacturing, of merchandising, of transportation and of finance must soon gain recognition. The establishment of business schools in our universities is a manifestation of the modern conception of business.

[1] An address delivered at Brown University Commencement Day, 1912. Published in "System," October, 1912.

The peculiar characteristics of a profession as distinguished from other occupations, I take to be these:

First. A profession is an occupation for which the necessary preliminary training is intellectual in character, involving knowledge and to some extent learning, as distinguished from mere skill.

Second. It is an occupation which is pursued largely for others and not merely for one's self.

Third. It is an occupation in which the amount of financial return is not the accepted measure of success.

Is not each of these characteristics found to-day in business worthily pursued?

The field of knowledge requisite to the more successful conduct of business has been greatly widened by the application to industry not only of chemical, mechanical and electrical science, but also the new science of management; by the increasing difficulties involved in adjusting the relations of labor to capital; by the necessary intertwining of social with industrial problems; by the ever extending scope of state and federal regulation of business. Indeed, mere size and territorial expansion have compelled the business man to enter upon new and broader fields of knowledge in order to match his achievements with his opportunities.

This new development is tending to make business an applied science. Through this development the relative value in business of the trading instinct and of mere shrewdness have, as compared with other faculties, largely diminished. The conception of trade itself has changed. The old idea of a good bargain was a transaction in which one man got the better of another. The new idea of a good contract is a transaction which is good for both parties to it.

Under these new conditions, success in business must mean something very different from mere money-making. In business the able man ordinarily earns a larger income than one less able. So does the able man in the recognized professions — in law, medicine or engineering; and even in those professions more remote from money-making, like the ministry, teaching or social work. The world's demand for efficiency is so great and the supply so small, that the price of efficiency is high in every field of human activity.

The recognized professions, however, definitely reject the size of the financial return as the measure of success. They select as their test, excellence of performance in the broadest sense — and include, among other things, advance in the particular occupation and service to the community. These are the basis of all worthy reputations in the recognized professions. In them a large income is the ordinary incident of success; but he who exaggerates the value of the incident is apt to fail of real success.

To the business of to-day a similar test must be applied. True, in business the earning of profit is something more than an incident of success. It is an essential condition of success; because the continued absence of profit itself spells failure. But while loss spells failure, large profits do not connote success. Success must be sought in business also in excellence of performance; and in business, excellence of performance manifests itself, among other things, in the advancing of methods and processes; in the improvement of products; in more perfect organization, eliminating friction as well as waste; in bettering the condition of the workingmen, developing their faculties and promoting their happiness; and in the establishment of right relations with customers and with the community.

In the field of modern business, so rich in opportunity for the exercise of man's finest and most varied mental faculties and moral qualities, mere money-making cannot be regarded as the legitimate end. Neither can mere growth in bulk or power be admitted as a worthy ambition. Nor can a man nobly mindful of his serious responsibilities to society, view business as a game; since with the conduct of business human happiness or misery is inextricably interwoven.

Real success in business is to be found in achievements comparable rather with those of the artist or the scientist, of the inventor or the statesman. And the joys sought in the profession of business must be like their joys and not the mere vulgar satisfaction which is experienced in the acquisition of money, in the exercise of power or in the frivolous pleasure of mere winning.

It was such real success, comparable with the scientist's, the inventor's, the statesman's, which marked the career of William H. McElwain of Boston, who died in 1908 at the age of forty-one. He had been in business on his own account but thirteen years. Starting without means, he left a fortune, all of which had been earned in the competitive business of shoe manufacturing, without the aid of either patent or trademark. That shows McElwain did not lack the money-making faculty. His company's sales grew from $75,957 in 1895 to $8,691,274 in 1908.

He became thus one of the largest shoe
manufacturers in the world. That shows he
did not lack either ambition or organizing ability. The working capital required for this
rapidly growing business was obtained by him
without surrendering to outside investors or to
bankers any share in the profits of business: all
the stock in his company being owned either by
himself or his active associates. That shows
he did not lack financial skill.

But this money-making faculty, organizing
ability and financial skill were with him servants, not masters. He worked for nobler ends
than mere accumulation or lust of power. In
those thirteen years McElwain made so many
advances in the methods and practices of the
long-established and prosperous branch of industry in which he was engaged, that he may be
said to have revolutionized shoe manufacturing.
He found it a trade; he left it an applied science.

This is the kind of thing he did: In 1902 the
irregularity in the employment of the shoe
worker was brought to his attention. He became greatly impressed with its economic waste,
with the misery to the workers and the demoralization which attended it. Irregularity of employment is the worst and most extended of
industrial evils. Even in fairly prosperous

times the workingmen of America are subjected
to enforced idleness and loss of earnings, on the
average, probably ten to twenty per cent of their
working time. The irregularity of employment
was no greater in the McElwain factories than
in other shoe factories. The condition was
not so bad in shoe manufacturing as in many
other branches of industry. But it was bad
enough; for shoe manufacturing was a seasonal
industry. Most manufacturers closed their factories twice a year. Some manufacturers had
two additional slack periods.

This irregularity had been accepted by the
trade — by manufacturers and workingmen
alike — as inevitable. It had been bowed to as
if it were a law of nature — a cross to be borne
with resignation. But with McElwain an evil
recognized was a condition to be remedied; and
he set his great mind to solving the problem of
irregularity of employment in his own factories;
just as Wilbur Wright applied his mind to the
aeroplane, as Bell, his mind to the telephone,
and as Edison, his mind to the problems of electric light. Within a few years irregularity of
employment had ceased in the McElwain factories; and before his death every one of his
many thousand employees could find work three
hundred and five days in the year.

Closely allied with the establishment of regularity of employment was the advance made by McElwain in introducing punctual delivery of goods manufactured by his company. Shoes are manufactured mainly upon orders; and the orders are taken on samples submitted. The samples are made nearly a year before the goods are sold to the consumer. Samples for the shoes which will be bought in the spring and summer of 1913 were made in the early summer of 1912. The solicitation of orders on these samples began in the late summer. The manufacture of the shoes commences in November; and the order is filled before July.

Dates of delivery are fixed, of course, when orders are taken; but the dates fixed had not been taken very seriously by the manufacturers; and the trade was greatly annoyed by irregularities in delivery. McElwain recognized the business waste and inconvenience attendant upon such unfulfilled promises. He insisted that an agreement to deliver on a certain day was as binding as an agreement to pay a note on a certain day.

He knew that to make punctual delivery possible, careful study and changes in the methods of manufacture and of distribution were necessary. He made the study; he introduced the radical changes found necessary; and he so perfected his organization that customers could rely absolutely upon delivery on the day fixed. Scientific management practically eliminated the recurring obstacles of the unexpected. To attain this result business invention of a high order was of course necessary — invention directed to the departments both of production and of distribution.

The career of the Filenes of Boston affords another example of success in professionalized business. In 1891 the Filenes occupied two tiny retail stores in Boston. The floor space of each was only twenty feet square. One was a glove stand, the other a women's specialty store. Twenty years later their sales were nearly $5,000,000 a year. In September, 1912, they moved into a new building with more than nine acres of floor space. But the significant thing about their success is not their growth in size or in profits. The trade offers many other examples of similar growth. The pre-eminence of the Filenes lies in the advance which has been made in the nature, the aims and the ideals of retailing, due to their courage, initiative, persistence and fine spirit. They have applied minds of a high order and a fine ethical sense to the prosaic and seemingly uninteresting business of selling women's garments. Instead of remaining petty tradesmen, they have become, in every sense of the word, great merchants.

The Filenes recognized that the function of retail distribution should be undertaken as a social service, equal in dignity and responsibility to the function of production; and that it should be studied with equal intensity in order that the service may be performed with high efficiency, with great economy and with nothing more than a fair profit to the retailer. They recognized that to serve their own customers properly, the relations of the retailer to the producer must be fairly and scientifically adjusted; and, among other things, that it was the concern of the retailer to know whether the goods which he sold were manufactured under conditions which were fair to the workers — fair as to wages, hours of work and sanitary conditions.

But the Filenes recognized particularly their obligations to their own employees. They found as the common and accepted conditions in large retail stores, that the employees had no voice as to the conditions or rules under which they were to work; that the employees had no appeal from policies prescribed by the management; and that in the main they were paid the lowest rate of wages possible under competitive conditions.

In order to insure a more just arrangement for those working in their establishment, the Filenes provided three devices:

First. A system of self-government for employees, administered by the store co-operative association. Working through this association, the employees have the right to appeal from and to veto policies laid down by the management. They may adjust the conditions under which employees are to work, and, in effect, prescribe conditions for themselves.

Second. A system of arbitration, through the operation of which individual employees can call for an adjustment of differences that may exist between themselves and the management as to the permanence of employment, wages, promotion or conditions of work.

Third. A minimum wage scale, which provides that no woman or girl shall work in their store at a wage less than eight dollars a week, no matter what her age may be or what grade of position she may fill.

The Filenes have thus accepted and applied the principles of industrial democracy and of social justice. But they have done more — they have demonstrated that the introduction

of industrial democracy and of social justice is
at least consistent with marked financial success. They assert that the greater efficiency of
their employees shows industrial democracy and
social justice to be money-makers. The so-
called "practical business man," the narrow
money-maker without either vision or ideals,
who hurled against the Filenes, as against Mc-
Elwain, the silly charge of being "theorists,"
has been answered even on his own low plane
of material success.

McElwain and the Filenes are of course exceptional men; but there are in America to-day
many with like perception and like spirit. The
paths broken by such pioneers will become the
peopled highways. Their exceptional methods
will become accepted methods. Then the term
"Big business" will lose its sinister meaning,
and will take on a new significance. "Big business" will then mean business big not in bulk
or power, but great in service and grand in
manner. "Big business" will mean professionalized business, as distinguished from the
occupation of petty trafficking or mere money-
making. And as the profession of business
develops, the great industrial and social problems expressed in the present social unrest will
one by one find solution.

THE EMPLOYER AND TRADES UNIONS [1]

Mr. Chairman and Gentlemen: —

I AM glad to be with you. A reunion of veterans is enjoyable, particularly so if the war has been successful — properly so if the right has triumphed, as in the recent struggle in which we were engaged.

Let me review the facts: —

Prior to February 1, 1901, the minimum wage of compositors in Boston was $15 per week. A three years' agreement then entered into between your association and the Boston Typographical Union No. 13 fixed the minimum weekly wage at $16 for the first year, and $16.50 for the two succeeding years. Shortly before February 1, 1904, the Union demanded that the minimum wage be further increased to $18. You offered an increase to $17 for the first year, and $18 thereafter. The Union rejected your offer, and ordered a general strike. On February 1, 1904, the compositors went out.

No principle of trade unionism was involved,

---

[1] An address delivered at the annual banquet of the Boston Typothetæ, April 21, 1904, for whom Mr. Brandeis had acted as counsel in a memorable struggle with the Typographical Union.

nor the question of increased wages for an indefinite period in the future. It was at most a matter of $1 a week for one year — the equivalent of what would be lost by each man in wages if the strike lasted just three weeks. To strike for such a stake was shockingly bad business. It was followed quickly by acts which also shocked the conscience.

The United Typothetæ had made a four years' contract with the International Printing Pressmen and Assistants' Union. This contract provided for arbitration of grievances, provided expressly against sympathetic strikes, and recognized expressly the open shop. In defiance of this agreement and in the face of the protest of Martin P. Higgins, the President of that Union, the Boston Typographical Union No. 13 undertook, by the promise of strike benefits, which in many cases exceeded the wages the men were receiving, to induce pressmen and feeders, who had no grievance whatever, to leave your employ. That was morally wrong. We believed it to be also illegal. You applied to the Supreme Judicial Court of Massachusetts for redress, and were accorded the protection of an injunction.

This was the beginning of the end; but the end itself came in a manner even more desirable. After the strike had continued five weeks, and the men had lost twice the paltry sum for which alone they struck, Mr. Lynch, the President of the International Typographical Union, and other members of its Executive Committee, came to Boston. They investigated the facts. They doubtless realized the hopelessness of the contest. They certainly realized the wrongfulness of inducing pressmen and feeders who had no grievance to go out in defiance of their contract. The strike was declared off — unconditionally. No promise of any kind was made to the compositors, pressmen and feeders who went out. The open shop was formally declared in every office. Many of the men who went out are still without work, and the strike benefits have ceased. The dynasty which for years has governed the Boston Typographical Union with unwisdom is tottering. The secretary has already resigned. The president, it is said, will not seek re-election.

So much for the past: what shall the future be? What should you do to make it an era of peace and prosperity? The answer involves a discussion of certain broad principles which, in my opinion, should govern the relations of employer and employee in all branches of industry, though in their application they would,

like every rule, be subject to exceptions more
or less temporary, dependent upon the peculiar
facts of the individual case.

First. Prolonged peace and prosperity can
rest only upon the foundation of industrial liberty. The peace which employers should seek
is not the peace of fifty years ago, when the employers were absolute masters of the situation.
The peace which the employees should seek is
not the peace of mediæval guilds, with their
numberless restrictions. Industrial liberty must
attend political liberty. The lead which America takes in the industrial world is no doubt due
to our unbounded resources; but of these resources none are so great as the spirit and the
ability incident to a free people. We lead the
world industrially, not so much because the resources of nature are unbounded, as because the
faculties and aspirations of men are comparatively unfettered. The prosperity of New England — this poor rich country — is ample evidence of this. We must have, therefore, for the
development of our industries, as for the development of our citizens, the highest degree of liberty attainable. Industrial democracy should
ultimately attend political democracy. Industrial absolutism is not merely impossible in this
country at the present time, but is most unde-

sirable. We must avoid industrial despotism, even though it be benevolent despotism. Our employers can no more afford to be absolute masters of their employees than they can afford to submit to the mastery of their employees, than the individual employees can afford to have their own abilities or aspirations hampered by the limitations of their fellows. Some way must be worked out by which employer and employee, each recognizing the proper sphere of the other, will each be free to work for his own and for the common good, and that the powers of the individual employee may be developed to the utmost. To attain that end, it is essential that neither should feel that he stands in the power — at the mercy — of the other. The sense of unrestricted power is just as demoralizing for the employer as it is for the employee. Neither our intelligence nor our characters can long stand the strain of unrestricted power. Every business requires for its continued health the *memento mori* of competition from without. It requires, likewise, a certain competition within, which can exist only where the ownership and management on one hand, and the employees on the other, shall each be alert, hopeful, self-respecting, and free to work out for themselves the best conceivable conditions.

Second. The right of labor to organize is recognized by law, and should be fully recognized by employers. There will be in most trades little probability of attaining the best conceivable conditions unless in some form a union of the employees exists. It is no answer to this proposition to point to instances of trade-union excesses and of the disasters which attended them. We believe in democracy despite the excesses of the French Revolution. Nor are claims of the trades unions disproved by pointing to the instances where the best results have been attained in businesses in which no trace of unionism existed. Wise, far-seeing employers act upon the spirit or the hint of union demands instead of waiting to have them enforced. "A word to the wise is sufficient." The steps in advance have been taken often for the express purpose of preventing trades-unionism from finding a lodgment, often, unconsciously, as a result merely of the enlightenment which comes with the necessary thinking that trade-union agitation compels. Such successful businesses are, indeed, the greatest triumphs of unionism; and their marked success is due in large part to the fact that they have had all the advantages of unionism without having to bear the disadvantages which, in their imperfect state, attend the unions. We must not forget the merits of unionism in our righteous indignation against certain abuses of particular unionists.

Most people admit the immense service which the labor unions have rendered to the community during the last twenty-five years in raising of wages, shortening of the hours of labor, bettering of conditions under which labor is performed, and protecting women and children from excessive or ill-timed work; but the services which the labor unions can render in the future are even greater than they have rendered in the past. The employer needs the unions "to stay him from the fall of vanity"; the employees need them for their own protection; the community needs them to raise the level of the citizen.

Strong, stable trades unions can best serve these ends. The leaders of strong unions only will adequately feel the terrible responsibility resting upon them. The leaders of stable unions only can get the experience essential to an adequate performance of their duties; and experience almost invariably makes the leaders reasonable and conservative. Only long service as a labor leader can give that knowledge of the employer's side of the controversy which is essential to its just and proper settlement. Peace and prosperity, therefore, are not to be attained

by any attempt to weaken trades unions. Our
hope lies rather in their growing strength and
stability.

At all events, the employer, whether he wills
it or not, has in most trades to reckon with the
union. What shall his attitude be?

Third. Employees are entitled to be represented by union officers. A short time ago it
was common for an employer not to "recognize
the union." That is, although he knew a large
number of his employees were members of the
union, he refused to negotiate in matters relat-
ing to the employees with its officers, on the
theory that the employer should deal directly
and only with his employees, and may not brook
the interference of an outsider. This plausible
but unsound theory has yielded generally to
facts and to reason. One hears little now of
employers arbitrarily refusing to deal with the
chosen representatives of union employees.
But, of course, recognizing that union officers
are the proper representatives of the employees
in any matter requiring consideration by the employer does not mean yielding to union demands,
any more than recognizing a customer means
conceding his demands.

How, then, shall the employer deal with the
union's representative when a demand is made

to which he feels he cannot accede, or when a controversy has already arisen? Many are ready with the answer: Arbitration; others again say: Conciliation. Arbitration and conciliation are each at times wise, but each involves the intercession of third parties. In arbitration it is the referee; in conciliation, the common friend. Ordinarily, neither is needed.

Fourth. Employers and employees should try to agree. A very able man, who taught the law of partnership at Harvard, once asked the class, "What shall be done if a controversy arises between partners?" The students suggested one legal remedy after another, — a receiver, an injunction, a dissolution. "No," said he, "they should try to agree." In the most important sense, employer and employee are also partners. They, too, should try to agree; and the attempt made in a properly conducted conference will generally be successful.

Nine-tenths of the serious controversies which arise in life result from misunderstanding, result from one man not knowing the facts which to the other man seem important, or otherwise failing to appreciate his point of view. A properly conducted conference involves a frank disclosure of such facts — patient, careful argument, willingness to listen and to consider.

Bluff and bluster have no place there. The spirit must be, "Come, let us reason together." Such a conference is impossible where the employer clings to the archaic belief commonly expressed in the words, "This is my business, and I will run it as I please." It is impossible where the labor representative, swaggering in his power to inflict injury by strike and boycott, is seeking an unfair advantage of the employers, or would seek to maintain even a proper position by improper means. Such conferences will succeed only if employer and employee recognize that, even if there be no so-called system of profit-sharing, they are in a most important sense partners, and that each is entitled to a patient hearing, with a mind as open as the prejudice of self-interest permits.

The potent force of right reasoning in such conferences can hardly be overestimated. If applied with tact and in the aid of right action, it is almost irresistible. But it must be used only in the right spirit and in the aid of right action.

Fifth. It is necessary that the owners or the real managers of the business should themselves participate in the conferences, partly because the labor problem requires the best thought available and the most delicate treatment, and partly because the employees feel better satisfied and are apt to receive better treatment when they are dealing with the ultimate authority and not with an intermediary. Such conferences are necessarily time-consuming, but the time cannot be better spent. They are as instructive to the employer as to the employees. We must remember that there are no short cuts in evolution.

The greatest obstacle to the success of such conferences is the suspicion of the labor representatives — a suspicion due partly to ignorance of the employer's actual attitude, partly to knowledge of individual acts of unfairness of other employers, and partly also to a belief, which is frequently erroneous, that the employer will get some advantage through his supposed superior skill and ability. Suspicion yields only to experience; and for this reason, among others, the conferences are most successful when participated in by labor leaders of long standing. The more experienced the representative, the better.

But conferences, though wisely conducted and with the best of intentions on either side, do not always result in agreement. Men fail at times to see the right; and, indeed, what is right is often in doubt. For such cases arbitration affords frequently an appropriate remedy.

This remedy deserves to take its place among the honorable means of settling those questions to which it properly applies. Questions arise however, which may not be arbitrated. Differences are sometimes fundamental. Demands may be made which the employer, after the fullest consideration, believes would, if yielded to, destroy the business. Such differences cannot be submitted to the decision of others. Again, the action of the union may appear to have been lawless or arbitrary, a substitution of force for law or for reason.

What, then, should be the attitude of the employer?

Sixth. Lawless or arbitrary claims of organized labor should be resisted at whatever cost. I have said that it is essential in dealing with these problems that the employer should strive only for the right. It is equally as important that he should suffer no wrong to be done unto him. The history of Anglo-Saxon and of American liberty rests upon that struggle to resist wrong— to resist it at any cost when first offered rather than to pay the penalty of ignominious surrender. It is the old story of the "ship money," of "the writs of assistance," and of "taxation without representation." The struggle for industrial liberty must follow the same lines.

If labor unions are arbitrary or lawless, it is largely because employers have ignominiously submitted to arbitrariness or lawlessness as a temporizing policy or under a mistaken belief as to their own immediate interests. You hear complaint, too, of lawless strikers in the legislature and in the city council; but, if lawlessness and corruption exist there, it is largely because the great corporations and moneyed interests have forgotten the good old maxim, "Not one cent for tribute, but millions for defence."

The world was aghast last summer at the disclosure of Sam Parks's corruption. The desecration of Labor Day by his glorification, after he had been sentenced to Sing Sing, was shocking to every sense of decency. This false loyalty of the unionists very properly alienated from trades unions much of the public favor which John Mitchell had gained for them. But, after all, Sam Parks's corruption and the terrible losses and suffering which attended the prolonged strike were largely the fruit of the employers' wrong-doing. Who bribed Sam Parks? The rich contractors, — pre-eminently the huge corporations on whose boards of directors sat many of the leading financiers of the country. They corrupted Sam Parks or fed his corruption, corrupted him either to get an undue advantage over their employees or over their competitors, or as a seemingly inexpensive way of meeting what they deemed to be unreasonable and extortionate demands. At last employers, employees, and a large part of the community paid the penalty. Fortunately, the world is so ordered that we must pay the penalty for our sins, be they sins of commission or omission, of doing wrong or of suffering wrong to be done unto us.

You may compromise a matter of wages, you may compromise a matter of hours — if the margin of profit will permit. No man can say with certainty that his opinion is the right one on such a question. But you may not compromise on a question of morals, or where there is lawlessness or even arbitrariness. Industrial liberty, like civil liberty, must rest upon the solid foundation of law. Disregard the law in either, however good your motives, and you have anarchy. The plea of trades unions for immunity, be it from injunction or from liability for damages, is as fallacious as the plea of the lynchers. If lawless methods are pursued by trades unions, whether it be by violence, by intimidation, or by the more peaceful infringement of legal rights, that lawlessness must be put down at once and at any cost.

Likewise industrial liberty must rest upon reasonableness. We gain nothing by exchanging the tyranny of capital for the tyranny of labor. Arbitrary demands must be met by determined refusals, also at any cost.

In our international relations we are told that the best assurance of peace lies in preparedness for war. This is equally true in the industrial world. The union has its strike fund. The employer must also pay in some form the premium for insuring an honorable peace. He has adopted long since the guaranty fund for his credits, the depreciation fund for his machinery. He should now adopt another reserve fund to guard him against the losses attendant upon strikes, and, above all, should so organize his business as to be less vulnerable to them. Known weakness invites arbitrary attack, as opportunity makes the thief.

These are the principles by which alone the labor problem can be satisfactorily solved. They are broad, indeed; for they are the eternal principles of

LIBERTY, FRATERNITY, JUSTICE, HONOR.

HOURS OF LABOR[1]

Mr. Chairman and Gentlemen:—

WHETHER in a particular business at a particular time the hours of labor should be materially shortened presents usually a grave question. Such a change, owing to competition, direct or indirect, may seriously threaten the prosperity or even the life of the business; or the demand for the reduction of hours may be coupled with other terms or conditions clearly inadmissible. In such cases strenuous resistance becomes the duty of the employer. But, however commendable the resistance of the employer to a reduction of hours may be in a particular case, we should all recognize that a short working day is in general essential to the attainment of American economic, social and political ideals, and our efforts should be directed to that end.

Mr. Gompers quoted some time ago the saying of Heine that "Bread is Freedom." The ancient Greeks, recognizing that "Man can-

[1] An address delivered at the first Annual meeting of the Civic Federation of New England, January 11, 1906.

not live by bread alone," declared that "Leisure is Freedom." Undoubtedly "A full dinner pail" is a great achievement as compared with an empty one, but no people ever did or ever can attain a worthy civilization by the satisfaction merely of material needs, however high these needs are raised. The American standard of living demands not only a high minimum wage, but a high minimum of leisure, because we must meet also needs other than material ones.

The welfare of our country demands that leisure be provided for. This is not a plea for indolence. Leisure does not imply idleness. The provision for leisure does not contemplate working less hard. It means ability to work not less, but more — ability to work at something besides bread-winning — ability to work harder while working at bread-winning, and ability to work more years at bread winning. We need leisure, among other reasons, because with us every man is of the ruling class. Our education and condition of life must be such as become a ruler. Our great beneficent experiment in democracy will fail unless the people, our rulers, are developed in character and intelligence.

Now consider what, particularly in our large cities, the chance for such development is for men and women who are required regularly to work ten or even nine hours a day. A nine-hour work-day means, including the noon hour, ten hours at the factory or workshop. That means in Boston for most of those who live in the suburbs eleven or twelve hours devoted to the workshop and getting to and from it. When you add the time necessarily spent at breakfast and supper, dressing and undressing, house work, shopping and sleep, you find that at least twenty-one of the twenty-four hours are devoted to *subsistence* and a small fraction of the day is left for *living*, even if after the long work day one is in a condition mentally and physically to really live.

To attain proper development of character, mind and body, a short working day is essential, and the eight-hour day is in most occupations and for most people not too short. For the exceptional occupation and for the exceptional man in any occupation, no general rule is required; and right thinking on this subject cannot be aided by reference to such exceptional instances. Most professions, many positions in business, and some in trades fall within the class of excepted occupations. Good work in such occupations almost necessarily brings with it joy, because it implies development of

faculties and, ordinarily, pecuniary advancement. In every occupation there are such possibilities for the exceptional man. But in most
industrial occupations — in the unskilled trades
and in many so-called skilled trades — the
limits of development and of financial success
for any individual are soon reached, and consequently there is little joy in such work except
as compared with the hours of idleness, or such
satisfaction as comes to the needy in securing
the means of subsistence.

And what is necessary to living as distinguished from subsisting?

In the first place, bodily health is necessary; that is, not merely freedom from illness,
but continued physical ability to work hard.
For those engaged in the more favored occupations, like the professions, and the higher positions in business and some trades, such health,
including the postponement of old age, has been
measurably attained by better conditions of
living, and notably by outdoor recreation.
What has been found necessary for continued
health and working capacity for those engaged
in these favored occupations we should seek
to make attainable for all our citizens. The
burden and waste to the community and to the
individual, and the suffering attendant upon

sickness and premature superannuation, may be and should be lessened by a shortening of the hours of labor so as to permit of proper out-door recreation.

In the second place, mental development is necessary. Massachusetts, recognizing the education of her citizens to be an essential condition of a free and prosperous people, has made compulsory the schooling of her children to the age of fourteen, has prohibited their working in manufacturing or mercantile establishments under the age of fourteen, and has withheld the right to vote from illiterate adults as inexorably as from idiots. But the intellectual development of citizens may not be allowed to end at fourteen. With most people whose minds have really developed, the age of fourteen is rather the beginning than the end of the educational period. The educational standard required of a democracy is obviously high. The citizen should be able to comprehend among other things the many great and difficult problems of industry, commerce and finance, which with us necessarily become political questions. He must learn about men as well as things.

In this way only can the Commonwealth be saved from the pitfalls of financial schemers on the one hand or of ambitious demagogues on the other. But for the attainment of such an education, such mental development, it is essential that the education shall be continuous throughout life; and an essential condition of such continuous education is free time, that is, leisure — and leisure does not imply merely a time for rest, but free time when body and mind are sufficiently fresh to permit of mental effort. There is full justification for the common practice in trades of charging at the rate of fifty per cent additional for work in excess of the regular hours. Indeed, I doubt whether that rate of pay is not often grossly inadequate to compensate for what it takes out of the employee. An extra hour of labor may render useless those other hours which might have been devoted to development, or to the performance of other duties, or to pleasure. The excess load is wasteful with man as well as with horses or vehicles or machinery. Whether the needed education of the citizens is to be given in classes or from the political platform, in the discussion of the lodges or in the trades unions, or is to be gained from the reading of papers, periodicals, or books, freshness of mind is imperative; and to the preservation of freshness of mind a short work day is for most people essential.

Bodily and mental health and development will furthermore tend to promote innocent, rational pleasures and, in general, better habits of living. Such conditions will tend to lessen the great curse of drink, and with it some of the greatest burdens of the individual and of society.

It is, of course, no answer to the plea for a shorter work day to say that the leisure resulting from shorter hours may not be profitably employed. The art of using leisure time, like any other, must be learned; but it is certain that the proper use of leisure, as of liberty, can never be attained except by those who have the opportunity of leisure or of liberty.

Nor is it an answer to the plea for a shorter work day to say that most workingmen secure a certain amount of free time through the irregularity of their work. Such free time is literally time lost. Such irregular excessive free time presents an even greater evil than that of excessive work.

Although the reduction of the hours of labor is clearly desirable, it may, as already stated, be impossible, on account of competition or other cause, to grant the reduction at a particular time in a particular business. But in my opinion employers are apt to exaggerate the resulting loss of earnings, at least in the long run. Greater freshness, better health and mental development that go with shorter hours may be relied upon within reasonable limits to make up, in many businesses at least, in part, for a shortening of working time, where the employer receives, as he should, the full co-operation of the employees to secure the largest possible production.

Obviously no limitation should be imposed upon the output of the individual, nor any rule be insisted upon by the employees which would hamper the most efficient use of machinery. Such arbitrary restrictions are wasteful and uneconomic at all times, and necessarily act as a brake on the movement towards shorter hours. The natural gain in vigor and working efficiency on the part of the employee should be allowed to show itself in the shop results. If this gain in potential efficiency is nullified by artificial limitations on what and how much a man shall do, with the facilities placed at his disposal, the decrease in working time must inevitably mean increased cost, without either economic or moral justification, and under such circumstances the employer has no other course open to him than that of resistance to any attempt to reduce the working time.

If in any case we should find that, despite

the fullest co-operation of employees, the reduced working time results in immediate economic loss, the welfare of our democratic community compels us to work nevertheless for a reasonably short work day as a condition essential to the making of good citizens.

ORGANIZED LABOR AND EFFICIENCY[1]

THE assertion that American prosperity is due to our great natural resources is only partly true. The fertile fields of the West would have brought us little wealth, but for mechanical science, and the development of agricultural machinery which eliminates waste in human labor.

In New England, particularly, our necessities and not our resources were the real cause of our prosperity. A poor soil drove us to manufacturing. High wages necessitated the saving of human labor and became the mother of our inventions, giving us labor-saving machinery. That the people of the East have not attained even greater general well-being is due, in large part, to the fact that the supply of foreign low-priced workingmen made it possible to meet the demand for higher wages by means other than the elimination of labor waste. Human nature, like the in-

[1] An Address before The Boston Central Labor Union on April 2, 1911. Published in "The Survey," April 22, 1911.

animate, seeks the path of least resistance. To think hard and persistently is painful. The path of the pioneer is beset with obstacles. It was easier to tap the inexhaustible foreign labor supply than to devise and to introduce better methods and better management. Instead of keeping down the labor cost by eliminating unnecessary human effort and increasing the productivity of the individual, we met the workingman's demand for higher wages by increasing the supply of workers. Instead of conserving the workingmen, we accepted the substitutes for those who had been incapacitated by disease or accident resulting from excessive toil or improper conditions of employment.

Fortunately a new necessity has intervened: the awakened social sense of the community, with its longing for a truer democracy. This great ethical movement for real brotherhood of man reinforces the demand of the workingman for wages, hours and conditions which will permit of his living according to those higher standards essential to life, health and the performance of the duties of citizenship in a democracy. These new and increasing demands have created a new necessity for economy in production. And scientific management comes prepared to relieve that necessity by a revolution in industry comparable only to that effected in the transition from hand labor to machinery.

It is important that the scope and incidents of scientific management be not misunderstood.

So much has been said of increasing the efficiency of labor that the importance of increasing the efficiency of materials, of plant, of working capital, and of improving service has not been fully appreciated. And yet the economies and the profits arising from the scientific handling of those factors in business are probably, in the aggregate at least, as great as from the increased efficiency of labor itself.

Saving the waste in materials is attained in part through securing that article which is determined by scientific tests to be best adapted to the needs; and incidentally proper tests tend to eliminate dishonesty in purchasing. Saving of waste in material is attained in part by so utilizing it that a lower cost results, even if the article was purchased at a higher price. It is attained in part through proper methods of storage and accounting, which prevent actual waste of the material itself and dishonesty in its use.

Saving in plant is attained not only by adopting the best, but by so equalizing, plac-

ing and using the equipment through careful
planning as to secure practically its full use
all the time; thus reducing the capital invested upon which charges for depreciation,
interest or rental, taxes and insurance, must be
earned.

Saving in working capital is attained by
so controlling and linking the quantity of
supplies necessarily carried, and so eliminating delays in the process of manufacture,
as to reduce materially the amount invested
in raw material and supplies and in work in
process.

Improving the service so as to secure certainty and prompt deliveries reduces expense
and annoyances, and vastly increases the suc-
cesses and profits of the sales department.

Scientific management seeks to do for industry systematically and comprehensively in
conserving effort, materials and capital, what
heretofore has been done sporadically and par-
tially. Its engineers refuse to recognize that
there is any legitimate sphere in industry for
ignorance or lack of skill. Ignorance and un-
skilfulness necessarily spell waste, — and waste
is sinful, whether it be due to lack of training, of selection, of equipment or of planning.

In discussing the efficiency of labor a construction altogether too narrow has been given by some to the term "labor." The labor to be made more effective is that of the managers and high-salaried officials quite as much as that of the wage-earners. Indeed, the increased efficiency of the wage-earner is not possible until the heavy demands which scientific management makes upon those controlling and directing the business, including superintendents and foremen, are fully met. Increased efficiency must begin with those higher up. This is of the essence of scientific management.

Some persons unfamiliar with the principles and application of scientific management have assumed that there is in it something hostile to labor, and particularly to organized labor. This is absolutely unfounded.

First! They have assumed that the aim of scientific management is "speeding up"; that it seeks to make the men work harder, thus exhausting the workingmen. Such criticism shows complete misconception of scientific management. Conserving human effort, and the man, is a fundamental tenet of scientific management. Among other things, it demands careful training of the workingman: and the employer's investment involved in that training creates a special incentive to the employer to retain his employee and to conserve his powers.

When Fred W. Taylor, with infinite patience and genius, discovered the laws by which a given quantity of pig iron might be loaded into a car or a given quantity of coal be shovelled by hand in a third or fourth of the time ordinarily taken, he was protecting his workmen, not exhausting them.

The larger production incident to scientific management is not attained by "speeding up." It comes largely from removing the obstacles which annoy and exhaust the workman — obstacles for which he is not, or should not be made, responsible. The management sees to it that the best possible way of doing the job is shown the worker; that is, the way which takes least time, which takes least effort, and which produces the best result. The management sees to it that the worker's machine is always in perfect order. The management sees to it that he is always supplied with the necessary materials. The management sees to it that the work comes to him at proper times, with proper instructions and in proper condition. Relieved of every unnecessary effort, of every unnecessary interruption and annoyance, the worker is enabled without greater strain to furnish much more in production. And under the exhilaration of achievement he develops his capacity.

Second: Closely associated with the erroneous idea that scientific management means "speeding up" is the objection to scientific management because of the bonus system. That objection assumes that scientific management *is* the bonus system. The protest of labor against the bonus system is in part well founded; because the bonus is apt to do more harm than good when applied otherwise than as a part of the system of scientific management. The bonus system is a common incident under scientific management; but it must not be supposed that it *is* scientific management. There has been a great deal of scientific management without the application of the bonus system at all. But it is an integral part of scientific management that the workingman should get a "square deal," that he should get a proper share of the profit which he aids in producing, that his achievement should secure an appropriate reward. And in practice it has been found that this can be done usually more fairly through the bonus system than by any other available method of compensation. But by the bonus system must be understood something very different from the bonus system which has been applied in many establishments to produce "speeding up." It involves these essential conditions:

1. A scientific investigation in detail of each piece of work, and the determination of the best method and the shortest time in which the work can be done.

2. A teacher capable of teaching the best method and the shortest time.

3. Reward for both teacher and pupil when the latter is successful.

Has anybody ever heard of the bonus system operating unfavorably to labor where these conditions have existed?

Higher wages, to be provided by the bonus system or otherwise, constitute but one of the ways in which scientific management will advance the condition of the laborer. The workingman needs, besides higher wages, among other things, shorter hours of work. What greater hope can there be for shorter hours than that afforded by scientific management, the purpose of which is to eliminate, in every way, waste of human labor? If the productivity of the individual man is increased, perhaps even doubled or trebled, there will come with it the possibility of largely reducing the hours of work.

We are agitating now for the eight-hour day already introduced in many industries and in the public service. We are far from attaining the ideal; but we should not forget that it is due to science in business, to the labor-saving machines which have already so largely increased the productivity of man, that we have been able to make some progress toward our ideal working day. A hundred or even fifty years ago the working day was from twelve to fifteen hours long in many industries in which it is now but eight or nine.

With higher wages and shorter hours, the greatest need of the working man is regularity of employment. Irregularity of employment creates hardships and demoralization of every kind. It is the most sinful waste.

The introduction of scientific management in business has, wherever applied, made regularity of employment its prime aim. It could not be otherwise; because irregularity is the most potent cause of waste, not only of labor, but of plant and of capital. The existence of irregularity of employment is one of the greatest reproaches to modern business. It proves

that the management has not done its part;
and the very essence of scientific management
is to relieve the workingman from these conditions and hardships which arise from the
failure of the management to do its duty.

Third: Again, some persons have expressed
their apprehension of scientific management, as
if it were inconsistent with, or at least hostile
to, unionism. This rests upon an entire misconception.

The essence of unionism is collective bargaining; that is, instead of the employer dealing individually with each employee, he deals
with a large body through their representatives, in respect to the rate of wages and the
hours and conditions of employment. Is there
not just as broad a sphere for collective bargaining in shops where scientific management
has been introduced as where it has not? Collective bargaining may fix the minimum wage,
be it by the day or by the piece; collective
bargaining may fix the bonus, if any: where
it shall begin; its rate of increase; and how
it shall be applied; may fix the hours of labor
and all the other conditions of employment
just as much as if the management were of
the old rule-of-thumb, chaotic type. Surely
it is not inconsistent with the principles of

collective bargaining that one worker may earn more than another; for in most successful unions, like the cigarmakers and the boot and shoe workers, most of the operatives are on piece work, and the earnings of some workers are double or treble those of others doing like work in the same shop.

Fourth: Again, some persons have objected to scientific management on the ground that it would throw workmen out of employment. This has not been the result, and will rarely be.

Scientific management undertakes to secure greater production for the same or less effort; but that does not mean that less people will have work to do. If only the same amount were to be produced, the same number of persons might well be employed to do it, if they worked less hours or less hard. But a more satisfactory answer is found in the fact that the amount of products which can be consumed will depend practically upon the ability to buy.

If goods can be purchased cheaper, more can be bought for the same money. And more will be bought; at least if wages remain the same or increase. The problem is exactly the same which was presented when the cost of transportation was reduced by substituting railroads for the stage coach, and the cost of goods was lowered by substituting machinery for hand labor. Has anyone ever known the demand for labor to decrease when profits were large? The demand for labor grows because the demands of the people grow with the ability to supply them.

Fifth: It has been suggested by some that scientific management will displace the inefficient. On the contrary, it helps the "inefficient" most.

Scientific management recognizes the right of those less expert in the work to advance to greater efficiency, and the importance to the employer of training his workmen to be competent. It therefore provides through the most practical teachers for careful training of men to work in the best manner and to develop habits of industry, instead of letting the "devil take the hindmost" and exposing the less competent to the probability of discharge. It supplies instruction, and offers to the teachers special incentives if they succeed in bringing up the hindmost.

The social gains to the workingman through scientific management are greater even than the financial. He secures the development and rise in self-respect, the satisfaction with his work, which in almost every line of human activity accompany great accomplishment by the individual. Eagerness and interest take the place of indifference, both because the workman is called upon to do the highest work of which he is capable, and also because in doing this better work he secures appropriate and substantial recognition and reward. Under scientific management men are led, not driven. Instead of working unwillingly for their employer, they work in co-operation with the management for themselves and their employer in what is a "square deal."

As stated above, scientific management offers the means of meeting our social demands. The great advance created by the introduction of machinery we permitted, in large measure, to be dissipated socially — instead of utilizing the opportunity fully to raise the standard of our civilization. Another great opportunity is offered us. Shall we seize it? And I think that means primarily, will organized labor seize it?

If the fruits of scientific management are directed into the proper channels, the workingman will get not only a fair share, but a very large share of the additional profits arising from improved industry. In order

that the workingman may get this large share
of the benefits through higher wages, shorter
hours and better working conditions, the labor
unions must participate in fixing those wages,
hours and conditions, and in determining the
application to the various businesses of the
principles of scientific management.   Unless
the workingman is so represented, there must
be danger that his interest will not be properly
cared for; and he cannot be properly represented except through organized labor.   This,
then, is the supreme opportunity for organized
labor.

Will you utilize it to the full?

THE ROAD TO SOCIAL EFFICIENCY [1]

THROUGHOUT the civilized world a developing sense of social responsibility has compelled the community to support in some manner its needy members, whatsoever the cause of their inability to support themselves.

In granting this aid we are passing from sporadic, emotional charity to organized charities, and from mere relief to preventive measures. We have learned that financial dependence among the wage-earners is due, in large part, to sickness, accident, invalidity, superannuation, unemployment or to premature death of the breadwinner of the family. Contingencies like these, referred to in the individual case as a misfortune, are now recognized as ordinary incidents of the lives of the wage-earners. And since our existing industrial system is converting an ever-increasing percentage of the population into wage-earners, the need of providing indemnity against financial losses from such ordinary contingencies in

[1] An address before the National Congress of Charities and Correction at Boston on June 8, 1911. Published in "The Outlook," June 10, 1911.

the workingman's life has become apparent. So sickness and death benefits and methods of compensation for accidents have been resorted to. But this partial workingman's insurance has served mainly in making clear the need of a comprehensive system which shall extend protection also to the wage-earners in case of invalidity, superannuation or unemployment, and to the widows and orphans left helpless by the premature death of husband or father. In this movement to establish a comprehensive system of workingmen's insurance, Germany, France, and latterly England have already advanced far.

The United States must follow on the same path, for the conditions which have led to the introduction of workingmen's insurance abroad are universal in their operation. Besides, the form and aims of our Government should lead us to action, as well as the sense of social responsibility. American democracy rests upon the basis of the free citizen. We accord (to the men) universal suffrage. We urge strenuously upon every voter the duty of exercising this right. We insist that the voter should exercise it in the interest of others as well as of himself. We give thus to the citizen the rights of a free man. We impose upon him a duty that can be intrusted with safety only to free men. Politically, the American workingman is free — so far as law can make him so. But is he really free? Can any man ‚be really free who is constantly in danger of becoming dependent for mere subsistence upon somebody and something else than his own exertion and conduct? Men are not free while financially dependent upon the will of other individuals. Financial dependence is consistent with freedom only where claim to support rests upon right, and not upon favor.

President Cleveland's epigram that "it is the duty of the citizen to support the Government, not of the Government to support the citizen," is only qualifiedly true. Universal suffrage necessarily imposes upon the State the obligation of fitting its governors — the voters — for their task; and the freedom of the individual is as much an essential condition of successful democracy as his education. If the Government permits conditions to exist which make large classes of citizens financially dependent, the great evil of dependence should at least be minimized by the State's assuming, or causing to be assumed by others, in some form the burden incident to its own shortcomings.

The cost of attaining freedom is usually

high; and the cost of providing for the workingman, as an essential of freedom, a comprehensive and adequate system of insurance will prove to be no exception to this general rule. But, however large the cost, it should be fairly faced and courageously met. For the expense of securing indemnity against the financial losses attending accident, sickness, invalidity, premature death, superannuation and unemployment should be recognized as a part of the daily cost of living, like the more immediate demands for rent, for food and for clothing. So far as it is a necessary charge, it should be met now as a current expense, instead of being allowed to accumulate as a debt with compound interest to plague us hereafter.

Few intelligent property owners omit to insure against fire. Everybody recognizes the fire insurance premium as a current expense. And yet the chance of loss by fire is very slight as compared with the chance of loss of earnings by sickness, accident or premature death. Every intelligent manufacturer makes in some form a regular charge for depreciation of machinery and plant. And yet the depreciation of man through invalidity and superannuation is no less certain, and frequently more severe, than the depreciation of machinery. Every intelligent manufacturer recognizes rent, interest and taxes as current daily charges which continue although his plant is shut down or operates at less than full capacity. The manufacturer makes allowance for this in calculating the cost of production as an extra charge to be met from the earnings of active days. But the cost to the employer of carrying an unused plant is not as great relatively as the cost to the employee of carrying himself and family while unemployed. The manufacturer who fails to recognize fire insurance, depreciation, interest and taxes as current charges of the business treads the path to bankruptcy. And that nation does the like which fails to recognize and provide against the economic, social and political conditions which impose upon the workingman so large a degree of financial dependence.

What sum would be required annually to provide an adequate system of workingmen's insurance cannot be determined from existing data. The cost would obviously vary greatly in different occupations and in different communities. An amount equal to ten per cent of current wages would go far towards relieving in many industries the distress now incident to sickness, accident, invalidity, premature death, superannuation and unemployment of the wage-earner. But it is certain that the proceeds of even so large a charge as ten per cent of the average daily wage would, under present conditions, afford merely alleviation of, and not indemnity for, the losses now attendant upon those contingencies in the life of the workingman. The cost of providing complete indemnity would probably reach an amount equal to twenty-five per cent of the average daily wage. For the premiums requisite to secure indemnity from losses incident to sickness, accident, invalidity, premature death or superannuation would probably aggregate fifteen per cent of the daily wage; while the average percentage required to indemnify for unemployment due to lack of work would probably rise above ten per cent.

This huge and apparently prohibitive expense should not, however, deter us from taking action now. It should, on the contrary, incite us to immediate and vigorous measures. Indeed, it has in it elements of great encouragement. It will disclose how vast the waste incident to present social and industrial conditions is. And when the extent of that waste shall have been determined and made clear to our people, a long step forward will have been

taken on the road to improvement and resulting social economy.

Some idea of the possibilities of improvement in this connection are indicated by the
following data.

Professor Irving Fisher has compared the
mortality record of the industrial life insurance
companies, which provide life insurance to the
workingmen in amounts of less than $500 on
the weekly premium plan, with the mortality
in the ordinary life insurance companies, in
which the policies average $1,000 or more.
The figures of deaths per year for each 1,000
persons insured are these:

Age.	Industrial Life Insurance Mortality (Metropolitan Life Experience).	Ordinary Life Insurance Mortality (English Experience).
20	10.5	7.3
25	14.1	7.8
35	17.2	9.3
55	35	21.7

The conditions under which that portion of
our population live and work who are insured
in the ordinary life companies are far from
ideal, and leave open a great opportunity for
reduction of the death rate. But here we have
an average death rate among the workingmen at their most productive age — twenty-
five to thirty-five years — which is nearly

twice as great as the death rate among those engaged in other occupations. And this high death rate of the workingman is that of the average insured workingman, not the death rate of those engaged in extra-hazardous trades.

Can there be any doubt that, if this heavier mortality had to be adequately compensated for by the State or the industries, and the insurance cost paid from current earnings, its causes would be adequately investigated and the evil conditions of living and working which produce it would be remedied? Society and industry would find how much cheaper it is to conserve than to destroy.

How near at hand the remedy for high mortality lies is illustrated by the experience of the model factory village at Bourneville, near Birmingham. While the average death rate for all ages in England and Wales in the years 1902 to 1907 was 15.7, the death rate at Bourneville was 6.3; and yet the occupations of the inhabitants of Bourneville were fairly representative of the whole country. Over fifty per cent of the workers were factory hands; thirty-six per cent were mechanics, carpenters, bricklayers and others of unclassified occupations; and about thirteen per cent clerks and travellers.

Professor Fisher concludes also that, on the average, every American is sick thirteen days in the year.

Possibilities of lengthening lives and of avoiding sickness and invalidity, like the possibilities of preventing accidents, will be availed of when business as well as humanity demands that this be done.

William Hard quoted Edgar T. Davies, the Factory Inspector of Illinois, as saying that in the year 1906 one hundred men were killed or crippled in the factories of Illinois by the set-screw, and that for thirty-five cents in each instance this danger device could have been recast into a safety device. The set-screw stands up from the surface of the rapidly revolving shaft, and as it turns catches dangerously hands and clothes. For thirty-five cents the projecting top of the set-screw could be sunk flush with the rest of the whirling surface of the shaft, and then no sleeve could be entangled by it, and no human body could be swung and thrown by it.

The South Metropolitan Gas Company, which established, in connection with its system of compensation for accidents, a system of inquiry into all accidents with a view to their prevention, reduced the number of accidents per thousand in seven years from sixty-nine to forty.

John Calder, of Ilion, New York, tells of the reduction of accidents in an American plant from a yearly average of two hundred to sixty-four.

Can there be any doubt that if every accident had to be carefully investigated and adequately compensated for, the number of accidents would be reduced to a half or a third?

And undoubtedly the paramount evil in the workingman's life — irregularity of employment — would yield in large measure to like treatment.

The New York Commission, in its recent report on unemployment, gives data from the trades unions showing that "organized workers lose, on the average, twenty per cent of their possible income through unemployment," and data from the charitable societies showing that "from twenty-five to thirty-five per cent of those who apply to them for relief every year have been brought to their destitute condition primarily through lack of work."

Some irregularity in employment is doubtless inevitable; but in the main irregularity is remediable. It has been overcome with great profit to both employer and employee in important businesses which have recognized the problem as one seriously demanding solution. Society and industry need only the necessary incentive to secure a great reduction in irregularity of employment. In the scientifically managed business irregularity tends to disappear. So far as it is irremediable it should be compensated for like the inevitable accident.

The social and industrial engineers will find much of inspiration and encouragement in the achievement of their fellow-engineers of the factory mutual fire insurance companies of New England.

The huge fire waste in America is a matter of common knowledge. The loss in 1910 was estimated at $234,000,000; and yet there is one class of property, in its nature peculiarly subject to fire risks, which was practically immune. Some 2,600 factories and their contents, valued together at about $2,220,000,000, and scattered throughout twenty-four States and the Dominion of Canada, suffered in the aggregate fire losses of about one-fortieth of one per cent of the value insured. The factories so immune were those owned by members of the so-called "factory mutuals" of New England. The cost to these factories for fire in-

surance and fire prevention in the year 1910
was only forty-three cents for each one thousand dollars of property insurance. Half a
century before, the cost of insurance to the
New England factories was $4.30, or ten times
as great. The record of the "factory mutuals"
of Rhode Island and of some other States is
similar.

Now, how has this reduction of fire insurance cost been accomplished? It was done by
recognizing that the purpose of these so-called
fire insurance companies is not to pay losses
but to prevent fires. These mutual companies
might more appropriately have been called
Fire Prevention Companies; for the losses paid
represent merely instances of failures in their
main purpose. In these corporations the important officials are not the financiers but the
engineers — men who rank among the leaders
in the engineering profession of America —
and aiding them is a most efficient corps of
inspectors.

The achievement of these factory mutuals —
the elimination of ninety per cent of the fire
risks — is the result of sixty years of unre-
mitting effort in ascertaining and removing
causes of fires, and incidentally educating factory owners and their employees in the im-

portance of providing against these causes. The premiums paid represent the cost of this advice, inspection and education as much as the cost of what is ordinarily termed "insurance."

The progress of the factory mutuals in reducing fire losses was relatively slow; but it has been steady, as is shown in the following table of net cost of fire insurance per $1,000 per year in two representative companies:

Years.	Boston Manufacturers Mutual Fire Insurance Co.	Arkwright Mutual Fire Insurance Co.
1850–60	$4.37	
1861–70	2.79	$3.37
1871–80	2.54	3.00
1881–90	2.27	2.16
1891–1900	1.44	1.54
1901–1910	0.68	0.69
Year 1910	0.44	0.43

Possibilities no less alluring are open to the social and industrial engineer. Will the community support their efforts?

Consider how great would be the incentive to humanize social and industrial conditions if the cost of inhuman conditions were not only made manifest, but had to be borne from day to day unless the inhuman conditions themselves were removed!

Mere description of the misery unnecessarily entailed by the inhuman conditions, mere statements of cost, however clear and forceful, will fail to secure the removal of these inhuman conditions in industry and in the life of our people from which this misery springs. But if society and industry and the individual were made to pay from day to day the actual cost of the sickness, accident, invalidity, premature death or premature old age consequent upon excessive hours of labor, of unhygienic conditions of work, of unnecessary risks, and of irregularity in employment, those evils would be rapidly reduced.

We need a comprehensive system of workingmen's insurance as an incentive to justice. We need it, "lest we forget."

OUR NEW PEONAGE:[1]
DISCRETIONARY PENSIONS

HALF a century ago nearly every American boy could look forward to becoming independent as a farmer or mechanic, in business or in professional life; and nearly every American girl might expect to become the wife of such a man. To-day most American boys have reason to believe, that throughout life they will work in some capacity as employees of others, either in private or public business; and a large percentage of the women occupy like positions. This revolutionary change has resulted from the great growth of manufacturing and mining as compared with farming; from the formation of trusts and other large business concerns; from the development of our transportation and other public utility corporations; from the marked increase in governmental functions; and, finally, from the invasion of women into industry.

As soon as we awakened to the fact that America had become largely a nation of employ-

[1] The substance of a discussion before the Stanley Committee, January, 1912; published in "The Independent," July 25, 1912.

ees, the need of a comprehensive provision for
superannuated wage-earners secured attention.
Given the status of employee for life, and
the need of an old age pension [1] is obvious.
The employee needs the pension because he
cannot — or at least does not — provide adequately from his wages for the period of superannuation.   The employers need a comprehensive pension system because, while the presence
of the superannuated employees in a business
seriously impairs its efficiency, the dictates
both of humanity and of policy prevent discharge unless their financial necessities are provided for.   The demand for a pension system
grows more pressing as businesses grow more
stable; for in older businesses there is a constant tendency to accumulate superannuated
employees.   The demand becomes particularly acute when businesses grow large as well
as old; for then it becomes difficult to provide
for the individual needs of the abnormal
employee.

As stated by the Massachusetts Commission on Old Age Pensions (January, 1910):

"The problem of dealing with the aged employee
is an urgent one in the modern business world. The

---

[1] The term "pension" is used throughout in its popular sense as
including old age annuities.

use of machinery and the stress of industrial employment have made it increasingly difficult for aged employees to hold the pace. The universal demand nowadays is for young men. Many concerns refuse to take on inexperienced men over thirty-five years of age. Moreover, men wear out faster under the increased strain. What to do with the worn-out workers, — that is the essence of the pension problem. To carry them on the pay roll at their regular employment means waste and disorganization of the working force; to turn them adrift is not humane. In the past, large employers of labor have tried to meet this difficulty in piecemeal fashion, by retiring aged employees on pensions in certain cases, or giving them light work, each case being provided for separately, on its own merits; now they are beginning to deal with the problem in a systematic fashion, by adopting a uniform method of retirement with pension.

. . . .

"The motives that have induced large corporate employers to provide retirement pensions are partly economic and partly humanitarian or philanthropic. Economic motives play the leading part. This thing has been done because it has been found to be good business policy. The economic gain from the pension system is twofold; it eliminates the waste and demoralization attendant upon the continued employment of old men who have outlived their usefulness; and it helps to promote industry, contentment and loyalty on the part of the working force."

Economically, the superannuation provision may be considered as a depreciation charge.

Every prudent manufacturer makes an annual charge for the depreciation of his machines, recognizing not merely physical depreciation, but lessened value through obsolescence. He looks forward to the time when the machine, though still in existence and in perfect repair, will be unprofitable, and hence must be abandoned. This annual charge for depreciation he treats as a necessary expense of the business.

From the point of view of the workingman the expense of providing old age pensions is a part of the daily cost of living. He should contribute while able to work to a fund which will sustain him when he ceases to earn. From the point of view of the employer, the expense of providing old age pensions is a part of the current expense of his business. He should pay as he goes the accruing cost of retiring employees who will become superannuated. If the wage is insufficient to enable the workingman to provide himself with a pension, it is not a living wage. So far as the cost of the old age pension is paid by the employer for the employees' benefit, it is in substance a part of the wage. So far as such a payment by the employer is for insurance against that waste and inefficiency in his establishment which would result from retaining superannuated employees, and for protection against that discontent which would result from discharging the superannuated without providing for them financially, it is a part of the business expense. Since the cost of making old age provision is thus either a part of the employees' daily cost of living or of the employer's daily business expense, it should be treated as a current expense, and may be likened to the premium for fire or accident insurance. Whether in the adjustment of relations between the employer and the employee this current cost of providing old age pensions should be borne wholly by the employer, or wholly by the employee, or jointly by both, is an open question; but European and American experience makes it clear that under our present industrial system some comprehensive financial provision for the superannuated worker is essential to social if not to industrial solvency. To neglect such a requirement is as dangerous as it is for the manufacturer to ignore the depreciation of his machines.

For the protection of the wage-earner it is obviously necessary that the right to a pension shall not depend upon his being in the employ of a particular concern. If his right to an annuity is dependent upon his remaining in a particular employ he loses all protection whenever he ceases to be so employed, whether he leaves voluntarily, or is discharged, or in case the concern discontinues business by failure or for other cause.

Adequate old age protection, therefore, cannot be secured to the wage-earner through the promise of a pension from a particular concern. He should have old age insurance which will protect the wage-earner in whosesoever employ he may happen to be when he reaches the period of superannuation. For the protection of the wage-earner it is likewise necessary that the pension system should confer an absolute right. No pension system can be satisfactory which makes the granting — or the continuance of a pension after it has been granted — a matter of discretion.

Germany, France, England and other European countries have undertaken to secure through government action old age pensions for those who work in private businesses. The system adopted in each of these countries differs in some respects from that prevailing in each of the others; but each system embodies the essential requirements referred to above; namely, *the pension is not dependent upon the workingman remaining in any particular employ, nor is it dependent upon the discretion of any individuals.*

In America the providing of old age pensions for wage-earners in private businesses is left wholly to private initiative. Many large concerns — railroads, public utilities, industrial and financial concerns — have established their own pension systems. Under substantially all of these systems the wage-earner receives no protection unless he remains in the company's employ until the age of retirement is reached, and even in that event the original grant and the continuance of the pension are, in large measure, discretionary.

Thus, the pension plan of the United States Steel Corporation, which took effect January 1, 1911, provides pensions only for those who have been in the employ of the company at least twenty years, and remain until the time for retirement; but no one has the *right to remain* in the employ:

Article 26. "Neither the creation of this fund nor any other action at any time taken by any corporation included under the provisions of the fund, or by the board of trustees, shall give to any employee the right to be retained in the service, and all employees remain subject to discharge to the same extent as if this pension fund had never been created."

Even if the worker has remained in the employ until the time fixed for retirement, and has served faithfully, he has no *right* to a pension:

Article 24. "The pension plan is a purely voluntary provision for the benefit of employees superannuated or totally incapacitated after long and faithful service and constitutes no contract and confers no legal rights upon any employee."

And a board of trustees, in whose selection the workers have no voice, and on which they have no representation, may refuse to grant them a pension or may terminate it after it has been granted, for what they in their discretion deem adequate cause:

Article 22. "Pensions may be withheld or terminated in case of misconduct on the part of the beneficiaries or for other cause sufficient in the judgment of the board of trustees to warrant such action."

The pension plan of most other corporations embodies similar provisions. Thus, the pension plan of the International Harvester Company provides:

Article 14. "Neither the establishment of this system nor the granting of a pension nor any other action now or hereafter taken by the pension board or by the officers of the company shall be held or construed as creating a contract or giving to any officer, agent or employee the right to be retained in the service, or any right to any pension allowance, and the company expressly reserves unaffected hereby, its right to discharge without liability, other than for salary or wages due and unpaid, any employee, whenever the interests of the company may, in its judgment, so require."

It has often been said by the corporations that one of their purposes in establishing a pension system is to "develop loyalty." But provisions like those quoted above suggest a purpose rather to *compel* than to *develop* "loyalty." The system is in effect a form of *strike insurance.* The pension is made dependent upon continuity of employment for a fixed period. The worker cannot receive a pension unless he remains in the company's employ until the date for retirement, and he has no right to remain in its employ, since the company reserves the full power to discharge him at any time, with or without cause. After a wage-earner has served a number of years and feels himself growing older, the prospect of a pension becomes a potent influence. He realizes that if he abandons his position or is discharged, he loses not only immediate employment, but protection for old age. He realizes also that the chance of securing other employment is greatly diminished by reason of his advancing years; diminished not because he is already old and less efficient, but because he will become superannuated sooner than a younger man, so that his employment by another concern will impose upon it or its pension system a superannuation burden sooner than if a younger man were selected.

Features in a pension system like those quoted above tend to make the wage-earner compliant. He can be more readily relied upon to prove "loyal" and not to "go out" even if others strike for higher wages and better working conditions. The "continuous employment feature" of the pension system tends thus to rivet the wage-earner to his employer, and the provision by which the allowance of a pension is made discretionary further insures "loyalty" of the wage-earner during his employment. An employee of the United States Steel Corporation advancing in years might well be deterred from hazarding the prospect of a pension by trade-union activity, or even by joining a union.

The tendency of such provisions in a pension system to destroy industrial liberty is the more potent because the system is being adopted quite generally by those trusts and other powerful corporations which are determined to eliminate trade-unionism. Indeed, in many cases the pension system was introduced as an aid to carrying out that labor policy. Individual employees, working under conditions which preclude collective bargaining, obviously lack industrial liberty so long as they are so employed; for they have no part in determining the conditions under which they work. After entering such employment, the only remnant of liberty remaining to them is the liberty of leaving it; and the features of the pension system just referred to undermine that remnant of liberty.

A pension system with such features must either prove a delusive protection or operate as a bribe to induce the wage-earner to submit to a new form of subjection to the corporation. A frank employer recently said: "By providing so liberal a pension we have bought from the employee the right to leave us." Such a use of the pension is obviously illegitimate. The legitimate need of the employer for a pension system is satisfied if the provisions protect him from the necessity of keeping superannuated employees on the pay roll. This need of the employer is equally satisfied whether the

employee retires on a pension or leaves the
employ before the age of retirement. In other
words, what the employer should seek to accomplish by the pension is merely to protect
his business from the incubus of superannuated
employees; and this purpose is accomplished
as to each employee if he leaves the employ before he becomes superannuated. If the workingman so leaves, he should in some form carry
with him the accrued right to a pension — the
proportionate value of the time service —
which would ripen into a pension if the workingman or his new employer paid the premiums
of later years. Under these private pension systems that part of the pension earned by years
of service is wholly lost when he leaves the
company's employ, whatever the cause.

Employers seek to justify provisions in the
pension systems like those quoted above by
the fact that the pension fund is contributed
wholly by the employer. But this fact furnishes
no justification. The employer should not be
permitted, even at his own expense, to establish
a pension system which tends to rob the workingman of his little remaining industrial liberty. A practice bearing such fruits is clearly
against public policy. Many of our States
have, in aid of industrial liberty, prohibited

the employers from making it a condition of employment that their employees should agree not to join a labor union. It may become necessary to apply a similar prohibition against features in private pension schemes which have a tendency to unduly abridge the liberty of the individual workingman.

The Massachusetts savings insurance banks, and several of the life insurance companies, afford employers facilities for establishing pension systems which are free from the objections discussed above. From such insurance concerns there can be purchased for each employee an old age annuity which (subject to due premium payments) confers upon the holder an absolute right to the annuity, and which is equally effective in whosesoever employ the annuitant is, or if he be without an employer.

The premiums on such an annuity policy could be made payable at frequent intervals, say monthly, so that if payable by the employee they would not be too large to be borne, and if payable by the employer, they may be figured as a part of the current wage or expense. The policy should preferably be taken out while the wage-earner is young, so that the current premium may be small; for the annual cost of old age insurance, like that of life insurance, be-

comes almost prohibitive when the policy is
not taken out until the insured is advanced in
years. If the policy is not taken out until the
wage-earner grows old, the premium will be so
large that, if payable by the wage-earner, it
could not be borne, and if payable by the employer, might discourage the annuitant's being
employed. Under the Massachusetts system a
separate annuity policy is issued for each employee, so that the employee can take the policy
with him when he leaves a concern. The employee can then pay the premiums himself until
another employer is found who is willing to
assume the charge as a part of his own system of providing against superannuation. The
workingman possessing such an annuity policy
taken out when young should meet with no
difficulty in securing employment solely on
account of advancing years; for the burden
on the new employer of providing against his
superannuation would be no greater than in the
case of a younger employee.

Every pension system should be contribu-
tory and co-operative; that is, the cost should
be borne partly by the employer and partly by
the employee, and preferably in equal shares.
The management of the pension system should
likewise be shared in by both employer and

employee. The system should also be obligatory; that is, when a system has been established, all employees should, so far as possible, become subject to its provisions; and both employer and employee should be bound to continue the system once established. For the present, however, it should be optional with the employer and his employees to establish a pension system.

The Boston and Maine Pension Act,[1] passed by the Massachusetts Legislature in 1909, contains suggestions for such an elective obligatory co-operative system. That act provides, among other things:

First. A pension system is established only in case the company by a majority vote of its directors and a two-thirds vote of the employees voting thereon decide so to do. When adopted by such votes the system becomes operative with the force of law upon all persons then or thereafter employed, except such as voted against establishing the system, and also within three months thereafter filed their written objections thereto.

[1] The act, which embodies the results of long negotiations between the company and the employees, was enacted May 29, 1909. On June 18, 1909, the Legislature of Massachusetts authorized the New York, New Haven and Hartford Railroad Company to acquire control of the Boston and Maine system. The New Haven management being opposed to the establishment of the pension plan, the Boston and Maine pension system has not yet become operative.

Second. The pension fund is supplied by monthly contributions from employer and employees in equal shares, the employees' share being deducted from wages and transmitted by the company to the pension fund.

Third. The management of the pension system is vested in a board of seven trustees, three of whom are selected by the company, three by the employees (who are formed into a pension association), and the seventh by the six so chosen.

Fourth. The amount of contributions to the pension fund is fixed as a percentage of wages. What percentage shall be assessed is determined by the trustees (subject to the approval of the directors of the company) up to an amount equal to three per cent of the wages, and can be fixed at a higher amount if approved by the directors and the pension association.

Fifth. Any one who remains in the employ of the company up to the time of retirement has an absolute right to a pension. Any person who ceases to be an employee prior to the time fixed for retirement retains the right to a part only of the accrued pension; that is, a person who leaves the employ voluntarily, or who is discharged, receives not the full accrued value of the pension at the time of so leaving, but only an amount equal to his own contributions. The act embodies in this respect a very objectionable feature, which was reluctantly assented to by the committee of the employees, as necessary to secure the consent of the company to the support of the bill, and in the hope that a more just provision might be later substituted.

It is upon these general lines, consistent with individual liberty and industrial democracy, that the American pension systems should be developed.

THE INCORPORATION OF TRADES UNIONS [1]

LEST what I say on the advisability of incorporating trade unions be misunderstood, it seems wise to state at the outset my views of their value to the community.

They have been largely instrumental in securing reasonable hours of labor and proper conditions of work; in raising materially the scale of wages, and in protecting women and children from industrial oppression.

The trade unions have done this, not for the workingmen alone, but for all of us; since the conditions under which so large a part of our fellow citizens work and live will determine, in great measure, the future of our country for good or for evil.

This improvement in the condition of the workingmen has been almost a net profit to the community. Here and there individuals have been sacrificed to the movement; but the instances have been comparatively few, and

[1] An address delivered at a meeting of the Economic Club of Boston, December 4, 1902, and published in the "Green Bag," January, 1903.

the gain to the employees has not been attended by a corresponding loss to the employer. In many instances, the employer's interests have been directly advanced as an incident to improving the conditions of labor; and perhaps in no respect more than in that expressed by a very wise and able railroad president in a neighboring State, who said: "I need the labor union to protect me from my own arbitrariness."

It is true that the struggle to attain these great ends has often been attended by intolerable acts of violence, intimidation and oppression; but the spirit which underlies the labor movement has been essentially noble. The spirit which subordinates the interests of the individual to that of the class is the spirit of brotherhood — a near approach to altruism; it reaches pure altruism when it involves a sacrifice of present interests for the welfare of others in the distant future.

Modern civilization affords no instance of enlightened self-sacrifice on so large a scale as that presented when great bodies of men calmly and voluntarily give up steady work, at satisfactory wages and under proper conditions, for the sole reason that the employer refuses the recognition of their union, which they believe to be essential to the ultimate good of the workingmen. If you search for the heroes of peace, you will find many of them among those obscure and humble workmen who have braved idleness and poverty in devotion to the principle for which their union stands.

And because the trade unions have accomplished much, and because their fundamental principle is noble, it is our duty, where the unions misconduct themselves, not to attack the unions; not — ostrich-like — to refuse to recognize them, but to attack the abuses to which the unions, in common with other human institutions, are subject, and with which they are afflicted; to remember that a bad act is no worse, as it is no better, because it has been done by a labor union and not by a partnership or a business corporation. If unions are lawless, restrain and punish their lawlessness; if they are arbitrary, repress their arbitrariness; if their demands are unreasonable or unjust, resist them; but do not oppose the unions as such.

Now, the best friends of labor unions must and should admit that their action is frequently hasty and ill-considered, the result of emotion rather than of reason; that their action is frequently arbitrary, the natural result of the possession of great power by persons not accustomed to its use; and that the unions frequently ignore laws which seem to hamper them in their efforts, and which they therefore regard as unjust. For these defects, being but human, no complete remedy can be found; but the incorporation of labor unions would, among other things, tend in some measure to correct them.

The general experience in this country, in respect at least to the great strikes, has been that success or failure depended mainly upon whether public opinion was with or against the strikers. Nearly every American who is not prejudiced by his own peculiar interests recognizes the value of labor unions. Nearly every American who is not himself financially interested in a particular controversy sympathizes thoroughly with every struggle of the workingmen to better their own condition. But this sympathy for the workingmen is quickly forfeited whenever the conduct of the strikers is unreasonable, arbitrary, lawless or unjust. The American people with their common sense, their desire for fair play and their respect for law, resent such conduct. The growth and success of labor unions, therefore, as well as their usefulness to the community at large, would be much advanced by any measures which tend to make them more deliberate, less arbitrary, and more patient with the trammels of a civilized community. They need, like the wise railroad president to whom I referred, something to protect them from their own arbitrariness. The employer and the community also require this protection. Incorporation would in some measure help to this end.

When, in the course of a strike, illegal acts are committed, such as acts of violence or of undue oppression, the individual committing the wrong is, of course, legally liable. If the act is a crime, the perpetrator may be arrested and punished; if it is a mere trespass, he may be made to pay damages, provided he is financially responsible; and if money damages appear not to be an adequate remedy, an injunction against the wrongful acts may be granted by a court of equity. If the injunction is disobeyed, the defendant may be imprisoned for contempt.

Now, it seems to be a common belief in this country that while the individual may be thus proceeded against in any of these ways, the labor union, as such, being unincorporated, that is, being a mere voluntary association, cannot be made legally responsible for its acts. The rules of law established by the courts of this country afford, it is true, no justification for this opinion. A union, although a voluntary unincorporated association, is legally responsible for its acts in much the same way that an individual, a partnership or a corporation is responsible. If a union, through its constituted agents, commits a wrong, or is guilty of violence or of illegal oppression, the union, and not merely the individuals who are the direct instruments of the wrong, can be enjoined or made liable for damages to the same extent that the union could be if it were incorporated; and the funds belonging to the unincorporated union can be reached to satisfy any damages which might be recovered for the wrong done. The Taff Vale Railway case, decided last year in England, in which it was held that the Amalgamated Society of Railway Servants could, as a union, be enjoined and be made liable in damages for wrongs perpetrated in the course of a strike, created consternation among labor unions there, but it laid down no principle of law new to this country.

Numerous instances may be found in our courts where labor unions have been enjoined, and in our own State, more than thirty years ago, an action was maintained against a union for wrongfully extorting from an employer a penalty for having used the product of "scab" labor. But while the rules of legal liability apply fully to the unions, though unincorporated, it is, as a practical matter, more difficult for the plaintiff to conduct the litigation, and it is particularly difficult to reach the funds of the union with which to satisfy any judgment that may be recovered. There has consequently arisen, not a legal, but a practical immunity of the unions, as such, for most wrongs committed.

This practical immunity of the unions from legal liability is deemed by many labor leaders a great advantage. To me it appears to be just the reverse. It tends to make officers and members reckless and lawless, and thereby to alienate public sympathy and bring failure upon their efforts. It creates on the part of the employers, also, a bitter antagonism, not so much on account of lawless acts as from a deep-rooted sense of injustice, arising from the feeling that while the employer is subject to law, the union holds a position of legal irresponsibility.

This practical immunity of the labor unions from suit or legal liability is probably largely responsible for the existence of the greatest grievances which labor unions consider they have suffered at the hands of the courts; that is, the so-called "government by injunction." It has come about in this way: An act believed to be illegal is committed during a strike. If that act is a crime, a man may be arrested, but in no case can he be convicted of a crime except on proof beyond a reasonable doubt and a verdict of the jury, and on every jury there is apt to be some one favorable to the defendant. Many acts, however, may be illegal which are not criminal, and for these the only remedy at law is a civil action for damages; but as the defendant is usually financially irresponsible, such action would afford no remedy.

The courts, therefore, finding acts committed or threatened, for which the guilty parties cannot be punished as for a crime, and cannot be made to pay damages by way of compensation, have been induced to apply freely, perhaps too freely, the writ of injunction. They have granted, in many instances, this writ according to the practices of the court of equity upon preliminary application, wholly *ex parte*, and upon affidavits, without any chance of cross-examination. If the courts had been dealing with a responsible union instead of with irresponsible defendants, they would, doubtless in many of the cases, have refused to interfere by injunction and have resolved any doubts in favor of the defendants instead of the plaintiffs.

In another respect, also, this practical immunity of the unions has been very dearly bought: Nearly every large strike is attended by acts of flagrant lawlessness. The employers, and a large part of the public, charge these acts to the unions. In very many instances the unions are entirely innocent. Hoodlums, or habitual criminals, have merely availed themselves of a convenient opportunity for breaking the law, in some instances even incited thereto by employers desiring to turn public opinion against the strikers. What an immense gain would come to the unions from a full and fair trial of such charges if the innocence of the unions were established, and perhaps even the guilt of an employer! And such a trial would almost necessarily be had before a jury, upon oral testimony, with full opportunity of cross-examination; whereas now, nearly every important adjudication involving the alleged action of unions is made upon application to a judge sitting alone, and upon written affidavits, without the opportunity of cross-examination.

It has been objected by some of the labor leaders that incorporation of the unions would expose to loss the funds which have been collected as insurance against sickness, accident and enforced idleness; that these funds might be reached to satisfy claims made for wrongs alleged to have been committed by the union. I can conceive of no expenditure of money by a union which could bring so large a return as the payment of compensation for some wrong actually committed by it. Any such payment would go far in curbing the officers and members of the union from future transgression of the law, and it would, above all, establish the position of the union as a responsible agent in the community, ready to abide by the law. This would be of immense advantage to the union in all its operations.

Again, it has been urged that the incorporation of the union would lead to a multiplication of lawsuits, which would involve the union in great expense; but the expense of conducting such litigation would be insignificant as compared with the benefits which would result to the union from holding a recognized and responsible position in the community.

Again, it has been urged that the unions would not fear litigation if justice were promptly administered; but that it was the dragging out of litigation which was to be apprehended. I take it that, so far as the unions have suffered from the administration of the law, it has not been from delays but from precipitancy. They have suffered at times in the granting of preliminary injunctions, injunctions which have been more readily granted because of the irresponsible position of the defendants.

Again, it has been urged that the unions might be willing to submit themselves readily to suit if the rules of law, as now administered by the courts, were not unjust to labor. I am inclined to think that there have been rendered in this country many decisions which do unduly restrict the activity of the unions. But the way to correct the evil of an unjust decision is not to evade the law but to amend it. The unions should take the position squarely that they are amenable to law, prepared to take the consequences if they transgress, and thus show that they are in full sympathy with the spirit of our people, whose political system rests upon the proposition that this is a government of law, and not of men.

HOW BOSTON SOLVED THE GAS PROBLEM[1]

SHALL the public utilities be owned by the public? — is a question pressing for decision in nearly every American city.

To aid in its proper solution the National Civic Federation began about two years ago a comprehensive investigation of representative American and British gas, water, electric light and street railway plants, with a view to comparing the advantages and disadvantages of private and public ownership. The opinions of the experts upon the data so collected appear to be widely divergent and to indicate, so far as they can be reconciled at all, that neither private nor public ownership, as ordinarily practiced, is wholly satisfactory.

While this investigation was proceeding, Massachusetts entered, in connection with the Boston gas supply, upon an experiment, new in America, which may lead to the best practical solution of the public-utilities problem. The new Boston system creates substantially a

[1] Published in "American Review of Reviews," November, 1907.

partnership between the public and the stockholders of the gas company — a partnership in
which the public will secure an ever-increasing
share of the profits of the business.

This system has already given to Boston
eighty-cent gas, although Boston is located many
hundred miles from the mines which supply its
coal. Eighty cents is a lower price for gas than
is actually enjoyed by any other city in the
United States, except a few within the coal
and oil region, like Cleveland or Wheeling, and
Redlands and Santa Ana, Cal. Even in those
cities the price is not lower than seventy-five
cents — a price which Boston may reasonably
expect to attain soon. For, during the two years
ending July 1, 1907, four reductions in price each
of five cents have been made. To have reduced
the price of gas twenty per cent during that
period of generally rising prices in labor and
materials is certainly a notable achievement.
The most recent reductions in price were the
wholly voluntary acts of the company, made
under wise laws framed in the interest both of
the public and of the stockholders. The saving
to the gas consumer by these reductions was in
the first year $265,404.55, in the second year
$565,725.60, and will be in the third (the cur-
rent) year about $800,000.

That this saving to the consumer was not attained by a sacrifice of the interests of the stockholder may be inferred from the market price of the stock of the association which controls the gas company. In the two years following the legislation of 1905, a period in which most other stocks depreciated largely, the common stock of the Massachusetts Gas Companies rose from 44½ to 57½; and even in the severe stock depression of September, 1907, this stock was firm at 52.

Compare with the results of the Boston experiment the attempt in New York City made at about the same time to reduce the price of gas from one dollar to eighty cents by legislative fiat and the compulsory orders of the State commission. The New York company contended that the law was unconstitutional; the federal court issued an injunction; the consumer still pays out one dollar for each one thousand feet of gas; and the market price of the stock of the Consolidated Gas Company of New York fell during the same period of two years from 200 to 118, and in September, 1907, to 96 ¾.

But Boston has reaped from the sliding-scale system as applied under President Richards' administration of the company far more than cheaper gas and higher security values. It has

been proved that a public-service corporation
may be managed with political honesty, and
yet successfully, and that its head may become
a valuable public servant. The officers and
employees of the gas company now devote themselves strictly to the business of making and distributing gas, instead of dissipating their abilities, as heretofore, in lobbying and political
intrigue. As a result, gas properties which
throughout the greater part of twenty years
had been the subject of financial and political
scandals, developing ultimately bitter hostility
on the part of the people, are now conducted
in a manner so honorable as to deserve and to
secure the highest public commendation.

The passage of the Sliding Scale Act of 1906
marked the close of the campaign upon which
the Public Franchise League entered in 1903.
All Massachusetts gas companies had since
1885 been subject to the supervision of a State
commission with very broad powers, including
that of fixing prices. New securities could be
issued only with the commission's approval.
For many years stringent laws prohibiting
stock-watering had been in force. While these
laws are of great value and have protected
Massachusetts from many of the evils of corporate management from which other States

have suffered, dissatisfaction with conditions
from time to time prevailing in connection with
the Boston gas supply was persistent and well
founded. Boston tried successively "regulated"
monopoly, competition and the combination of
gas companies. The service was poor and the
management unprogressive. The price of gas,
which after a strenuous contest had been reduced in parts of Boston to one dollar in 1893,
appeared to be immutable.

The application to the legislature made in
1903 for leave to consolidate the several Boston
companies then in combination afforded the
Public Franchise League its opportunity. Several minor provisions were inserted in the
consolidation act designed to protect the people's
rights, and the issue of capital by the united
company was limited to the net "fair value of
the plants and property of the several corporations as the same shall be determined" by the
gas and electric light commissioners, "without enhancement on account of the value of
franchises or earning capacity or on account of
exclusive privileges derived from rights in the
public streets."

The aggregate outstanding securities of the
constituent companies had a par value of only
$15,124,121 (of which $9,309,600 was stock and

$5,814,521 funded debt). But when, in 1904, application was made under the act to fix the capital, the companies claimed that the properties had recently cost the then owners over $24,000,000, that their replacement value was about the same amount, and that the fair value for capitalization should be not less than $20,-609,989.99. The Public Franchise League, on the other hand, contended that substantially any excess in value over the $15,124,121 represented not contributions by stockholders, but accumulations from excessive payments exacted from gas consumers; that in the reorganization of the business such value should not be capitalized; and that the Consolidated Company's capital stock should therefore be limited to the aggregate of the capital of the constituent companies then outstanding, plus such additional amount of stock as it might be necessary to issue at its estimated market value (which was above the par value) to provide funds for paying off all existing indebtedness. The league deemed the retention of the original capital so augmented of fundamental importance, mainly because the payment of a high rate of dividend on a small capital issue would tend to keep the public vigilant.

After a long and bitter struggle the gas companies, acting under the enlightened and able leadership of Mr. Richards, agreed, in 1905, with the Public Franchise League upon legislation which provided that the capital of the consolidated company should be limited to the aggregate par value of the outstanding stock and funded indebtedness of the constituent companies, to wit: $15,124,000; that the maximum price of gas in Boston should be reduced to ninety cents within twelve months after the consolidation was effected; and that the governor should appoint a commission to consider and report to the next legislature whether the adoption in Boston of the so-called London sliding scale system for "the automatic and interdependent adjustment of the price of gas to consumers and the rate of dividends to stockholders of gas companies" was expedient. The favorable recommendation of the minority of this commission, Messrs. James E. Cotter and Charles P. Hall, was supported by the Public Franchise League and the gas company, and on May 26, 1906, the Sliding Scale Act received Governor Guild's approval in spite of the strenuous opposition of both conservatives and radicals.

The Boston Sliding Scale Act, which embodies with some modifications the main provisions of the system widely used in England, provides as follows:

First. Ninety cents per thousand feet of gas (that is, the maximum price then actually charged by the Boston company) is made the "standard price" of gas.

Second. Seven per cent (that is, one per cent less than the dividend which was then being paid by the Boston company) is made the "standard dividend."

Third. The company is prohibited from paying more than seven per cent dividend unless and until one year after it shall have reduced the price of gas below ninety cents, and then may increase its dividend at the rate of one per cent for every five cents reduction in the price of gas.

Fourth. New stock can be issued only with the consent of the Gas and Electric Light Commissioners, and must be sold at auction at such minimum price and under such other conditions as the Commissioners prescribe.

Fifth. Provision is made for determining annually, and publishing in detail in the newspapers, the cost of manufacturing and distributing gas.

Sixth. After the expiration of ten years, the Gas and Electric Light Commissioners may, upon petition, "lower or raise the standard price per thousand feet to such extent as may justly be required by reason of greater or less burden which may be imposed upon the company by reason of improved methods in the art of manufacture, by reason of changes in prices of materials and labor, or by reason of changes in other conditions affecting the general cost of manufacture or distribution of gas."

A seven per cent dividend upon the capital of the consolidated company was equivalent to a return of about 4.35 per cent on the replacement value of the gas properties as testified to, and of their cost to the then owners. The "standard dividend," therefore, though nominally seven per cent, represented but a modest return upon the capital then recently invested, and was about $150,000 less than the aggregate amount then being paid by the several companies as return upon capital. Nevertheless strenuous opposition was made to the Sliding Scale bill on the ground that successive reductions in price would enable the gas company to pay very large dividends. The Public Franchise League recognized fully that after a few years' operation under the act much larger dividends would probably be paid than capital as capital is entitled to when employed in a business which is not only safe because it enjoys a substantial monopoly, but which also receives from the community without the payment of any compensation the license to lay and maintain its pipes in the public streets. The League insisted, however, that the proper aim of the public must be not to limit dividends, but to secure gas of good quality at low prices; that a limitation of dividends was desirable only when it conduced to that end; and that under proper conditions a reasonable assurance of the undisturbed enjoyment of large dividends might be the best method of attaining cheap gas.

The League therefore urged that the possibility of a large return upon capital offered under the sliding scale system should be regarded merely as an incentive to securing for the gas business the kind of management most likely to produce and distribute gas at the lowest possible cost, and thus supply an essential prerequisite to cheap gas. Protection against corporate abuses demands for gas companies strict supervision and publicity. Fairness demands that proper compensation be made in some form for the use of our streets. But no self-sustaining system of supplying gas can give to the people cheap gas unless it rests upon high efficiency in management.

The gas business has many of the characteristics of both manufacturing and merchandizing. Like other manufacturing businesses, it produces an article for sale. The cost of its produce is dependent largely upon the character and condition of the plant; upon the extent to which labor and waste-saving devices are adopted; upon the skill with which raw materials and supplies are purchased and waste or residual products are disposed of; and whether the plant is operated to its full capacity.

To an even greater extent than in most mercantile businesses, the pro rata cost of distribution of gas is dependent upon large volume. The distributing plant requires an exceptionally large investment. But the mains or pipes are rarely used to their full capacity. The interest, depreciation and maintenance charges are the same whatever the volume of sales. The inspection of meter, and many other charges, increase but slightly with the increase of sales. The pro rata cost of distributing gas diminishes largely, therefore, with the increase in the quantity sold. But, as in most mercantile businesses, the quantity of gas which can be sold in any of our large cities is dependent mainly upon the skill, energy, initiative and intelligence with which the business is conducted.

The demand for gas is not a fixed quantity. There is, undoubtedly, a minimum quantity which will be used under almost any conceivable circumstances. But limits can scarcely be set to the possible increase of its use in our large cities. Not only is there an ever-growing demand for intense artificial lighting of public places, stores and residences, but there is an almost limitless field now occupied by electric light, coal and oil, of which gas is the natural competitor. The limits of the use of gas in any city, therefore, will be set mainly by the skill, energy and initiative of those who manage the business and by the extent to which they appreciate the fact that increased use of gas will result from reduction in price, bettering of appliances and improving facilities.

A management possessing the requisite ability and skill for such a business and which would exercise the requisite vigilance and energy may be best secured by following those lines upon which the remarkable industrial advance of America has proceeded, the lines of intelligent self-interest. Those who manage our gas companies and other public-service corporations should be permitted, subject to the limitations stated above, to conduct the enterprise under the conditions which in ordinary business have proved a sufficient incentive to attract men of large ability, and to insure from them their utmost efforts for its advancement. These essential conditions are:

(a) The right to enjoy a fair share of the fruits of successful effort.

(b) The opportunity of devoting one's whole efforts to developing the business.

(c) The probability of pursuing for a reasonable time without interruption such business policy as may be adopted.

The Public Franchise League believed that the sliding scale system supplies in large measure these conditions essential to the successful conduct of our public services — conditions which are in no respect inconsistent with the restrictions demanded for a proper protection of the public interests. It believed also that the Boston company possessed in its president, Mr. Richards, a man of the character and ability required to make the sliding scale system a pronounced success. The results of the new law under his administration have happily confirmed the judgment of the League.

The rate of increase in savings to the gas consumer noted above — that is, from $265,-404.55 in the first year to $800,000 (estimated) for the third year — is due in large measure to the rapid successive reductions in the price of gas; and, obviously, further reductions will come more slowly. But further reductions may be expected, both because of the growing efficiency of the management, and the rapidly increasing consumption of gas.

The efficiency of the management is being promoted largely through the voluntary extension by the company of the sliding scale principle to its employees. Under this wise provision 681 employees receive, in addition to regular wages, a dividend on their wages, at the same rate as the dividend on capital stock paid to stockholders. And these 681 employees have either already become stockholders, or under the operation of the system will soon be such.

Even without further reductions in price, some increase in the saving to the people may be expected each year. For it is one of the great merits of the sliding scale system that while, upon reduction in price, the increased dividend is figured from year to year upon the same or substantially the same capital, the saving in price is practically certain to be figured upon an ever-increasing quantity sold. The reduction in price increases sales; and the increase of sales renders further reductions in price possible. The sales of the Boston company to consumers in the year ending June 30, 1907, were 23.73 per cent greater than in the year ending June 30, 1905 — the first reduction in price having been made as of July 1, 1905. The sales from July 1, 1907 (when the price was reduced to eighty cents), to October 1, 1907, were 16.6 per cent greater than that of the corresponding period of the preceding year. It is expected that the company will this year increase its dividend rate one per cent, calling for an additional payment to stockholders of $151,240; but the people will save in the current year (as compared with the standard price of ninety-cent gas) about $400,000. When the eighty-cent rate shall have been in force twelve months the company may increase its dividends, if earned, by another one per cent. But it cannot be so earned without a further increase in consumption of gas, which in turn must result in further reduction of cost and further increase of the amount saved by the people. The experience of the English companies under the sliding scale system shows that while, at the outset, the saving to the community and the amount paid on the increase of dividend were about equal, after a series of years the savings to the consumer were from three to seven times as great as the increase of dividends to stockholders.

If the demand for municipal ownership in America can be stayed, it will be by such wise legislation as the Public Franchise League has promoted and by such public service as Mr. Richards and his associates are rendering in the management of a private corporation.

LIFE INSURANCE: THE ABUSES AND THE REMEDIES [1]

Mr. President and Gentlemen: —

EIGHT months ago dissension among guilty officers of the Equitable Life Assurance Society first directed public attention to the conduct of the life insurance business. Since then the disclosures of financial depravity have aroused widespread indignation; but even now the importance of the subject is not generally realized.

OUR HUGE LIFE INSURANCE INVESTMENT

On January 1, 1905, there were outstanding in the ninety principal legal reserve or old line life insurance companies of the United States 21,082,352 policies. By these policies the lives of at least 10,000,000 of our people are insured. As these policies were taken out largely on the lives of husbands, intending to provide for widow and children, it is estimated that, on the average, more than four people

[1] Delivered before the Commercial Club of Boston, October 26, 1905.

are interested in each life insured. So we
have in all about 40,000,000 people, nearly
one-half of the total population of the United
States, directly interested in the conduct of these
ninety companies. The aggregate amount of insurance represented by these 21,082,352 policies was $12,928,493,754. That sum is more
than the supposed value of all the steam railroads in the United States which on June 30,
1904, was only $11,244,852,000. It is far more
than the par value of their aggregate bonds
and stocks held by the public, which was only
$9,585,467,711.

To provide for that insurance these companies received during the year 1904 new
money in the form of premiums aggregating
$498,303,279. That is, more than the aggre-
gate interest and dividends paid on all bonds
and stocks of our steam railroads held by the
public, which, during the year ending June 30,
1904, was only $465,872,674.

On January 1, 1905, these ninety insurance
companies held assets aggregating $2,573,-
186,639. That is, more than three times the
aggregate capital of all the 5,331 national
banks in the United States reporting June 30,
1904, which was only $767,378,148. The assets
of these insurance companies were nearly four-

fifths as large as the aggregate deposits in all the national banks, which were only $3,312,-439,841.

The total income of these insurance companies during the year 1904, including returns from investments, was $612,896,887. That is, more than the total revenue of the United States Government from all sources during the year ending June 30, 1905, which was only $543,423,859.24.

These figures, huge as they are, cover only a part of the direct interest of the American people in life insurance. Besides these ninety legal reserve companies, there are in the United States numberless assessment companies and fraternal beneficiary societies which provide life insurance. Their members are mainly wage-earners who cannot pay the high premiums exacted by the legal reserve companies.

But even the legal reserve companies insure mainly persons of small means, performing essentially the function of the savings bank. The large company advertises with pride its million dollar policies; but in 1904 the average size of the policy in the Equitable was $2,648; in the Mutual Life of New York, $2,351; and in the New York Life, only $2,076. In the Metropolitan and in the Prudential,

which join with the ordinary life insurance
business the specialty of insuring working
people, the average policy is only $183 and
$178 respectively. It will be seen therefore that
in spite of the large policies held by a few individuals, the life insurance of this country is in
the main held by what we term "the people"
— that large class which every system of business and of government should seek to protect.

THE COMPANIES' CONTROL OF QUICK CAPITAL

Such is the direct interest of our people in the
proper conduct of the life insurance business
— the interest primarily of the home. Indirectly the life insurance business affects our
industrial and political life no less vitally and
with perhaps even more far-reaching effects.
That influence results from the control which
the largest life insurance companies exercise
over our business and our political institutions
by means of the vast accumulation in a few
hands of the assets held as insurance reserve,
for deferred dividends or as surplus.

The aggregate assets of these ninety legal
reserve companies was, on January 1, 1905,
$2,573,186,639. Of that sum nearly one-half,
or $1,247,331,738, was held by the three lead-
ing Wall Street companies, the Mutual Life of

New York, the Equitable and the New York Life, not inaptly referred to as "The Big Three" and the "Racers." One billion two hundred and forty-seven million three hundred and thirty-one thousand seven hundred and thirty-eight dollars is a vast sum, but the control exercised by these three companies does not lie mainly in the size of the aggregate assets. It results from their character and from the conditions under which the funds are held. The $1,247,331,738 in assets held by these three Wall Street companies is a trifling amount as compared with the aggregate wealth of the country. What gives to the managers of these and allied insurance companies the control which they exercise over business is the fact that the larger part of the aggregate assets is quick capital. We have in the United States many other great aggregations of assets: in manufacturing, mining and commerce, the Steel Trust, the Oil Trust, the Beef Trust; in transportation, the Northern Pacific-Great Northern combination, the Pennsylvania system and the New York Central system. Even in combinations like these our people recognize a menace to our welfare and our institutions. But between the vast combinations of capital in manufacturing or transportation and the

accumulation of capital by the insurance companies there is this marked difference — the
capital of the manufacturing, of the mining,
and of the railroad companies is, in the main,
permanently invested in lands, buildings or
machinery, in rails, bridges or equipment, or
it is required for operating their properties.
The capital of the life insurance companies, on
the other hand, is mainly free capital.   The huge
manufacturing and transportation companies,
great and powerful as they are, are directly
dependent for their prosperity upon the prosperity of the country and the service which
they render from day to day to the people.
Furthermore they are constant borrowers.

The situation of the life insurance companies
is entirely different.   Except in respect to the
growth of their business, they are not dependent
for their prosperity upon that of the country.
Indeed, they derive certain benefits in times
of adversity.   While the securities they already
hold are not of a class to be imperilled, they can
purchase new securities to better advantage.
They are the creditors of our great industries,
with all the power which that implies.

Of the aggregate capital of these three leading life insurance companies there is invested
in real estate only 6.8 per cent.   The balance of

their assets is substantially quick capital. The larger part of it is invested in bonds and stocks, in collateral loans and money in bank. Moreover, these three companies — the Equitable, the Mutual Life and the New York Life — have in important respects co-operated with each other.

OTHER QUICK CAPITAL LESS

Compared with their quick capital, that of the great banking institutions of the country seems insignificant. The three greatest New York banks — the National City, the Bank of Commerce and the First National — had on September 30, 1905, in capital and surplus together, only $106,264,800. They had, it is true, in deposits $421,521,900, an aggregate about as large as the assets of a single one of these three insurance companies.

But over their deposits these banks have only a limited control. Twenty-five per cent must always be held as a reserve. Besides, substantially all deposits in banks and trust companies are subject to check. This right of the depositor to call for his money places a great restraint upon the use which it is possible for bank managers to make of the funds under their control; and these insurance companies are probably the largest depositors. On September 30, 1904, these three insurance companies had deposited in banks and trust companies $77,132,878. Such huge deposits secure to the insurance companies an effectual control over the banking institutions aside from the actual control which they hold through ownership of bank and trust company stocks.

The assets of the life insurance companies are substantially in the absolute control of the managers. Their officers know (except as to new business) with mathematical certainty approximately how much money they will be required to pay out each month for years to come; because the whole insurance business rests upon stability in average death rates. The insurance company may use most of its capital without danger of its being called by those for whom it is held.

Furthermore, while the amount of withdrawals from the banks from time to time is substantially equal to the deposits, the funds of these insurance companies are increasing at an alarming rate. To these three companies alone there was actually paid in premiums and income from investment in the year 1904, $254,-870,441.37. Only $111,161,905.25, or 43.61 per cent, was paid out by them to the policy-holders. The balance (except $7,000) was used either for expenses or accumulated for the future. In the four years preceding January 1, 1905, the gross assets held by these three companies increased $353,638,734.

The power of the financiers who control these Wall Street companies is further increased by close alliance with other life insurance companies. The largest of these allied companies — the Metropolitan and the Prudential — on January 1, 1905, had assets aggregating $216,659,984, and their rate of accumulation is even greater than that of the three leaders; for the Metropolitan and the Prudential draw from a larger public, mainly from the workingmen. In five years the assets of these two companies have more than doubled.

The "Big Three," with their lesser but powerful allies, join together in syndicates to insure the financing of the great manufacturing and railroad combinations, and furnish the weapons for our Napoleons of finance. The Northern Securities Trust, Morgan's attempt to perfect a monopoly of the railroads in the Northwest; the International Mercantile Marine, Morgan's attempt to monopolize a large part of the shipping of the world; Harriman's and Gould's ambitious plans — are made possible largely by the gathering of the savings of the people in the treasuries of these five insurance companies. How this financial community of interests operates in even the routine business of the companies may be seen from this: The Equitable held on January 1, 1905, besides $11,190,006 Government, State, City and County bonds and $3,708,945 Russian railroad securities (owned chiefly to comply with the requirements of foreign governments), bonds and stock of the aggregate cost of $192,849,290. Of these securities $184,740,473 — that is, all but $8,108,817 (or four per cent) — were of corporations in which either one or more of the directors of the Equitable were interested as directors or which were parts of systems controlled by such corporations.

When such facts are considered, it becomes obvious why the financiers who control these great insurance companies with their huge quick capital exercise a predominating influence over the business of the country. The economic menace of past ages was the church — the dead hand, which gradually acquired a large part of all available lands. The greatest economic menace of to-day is a very live hand — these great insurance companies which are controlling so large a part of our quick capital.

HOW POWER ENTRUSTED WAS ABUSED

Such is the power which the American people have intrusted to the managers of these large companies. How has it been exercised? Substantially as all irresponsible power since the beginning of the world: selfishly, dishonestly, and in the long run, inefficiently. The breaches of trust committed or permitted by men of high financial reputation, the disclosure of the payment of exorbitant salaries and commissions, the illegal participation in syndicate profits, the persistent perversion of sacred trust funds to political purposes, the co-operation of the large New York companies to control the legislatures of the country — these disclosures are indeed distressing; but the practice of deliberate and persistent deception of the public which the testimony discloses, though less dramatic, is even more serious. Talleyrand said, "Language was made to conceal thought." George W. Perkins would teach us that "Bookkeeping was made to conceal facts." Consider for a moment his situation. An important member of the most famous banking firm in America, and next to the Rothschilds the most famous in the world, confesses this:

The New York Life company, of which he is

the vice-president, held on December 31, 1903, an investment taken through his firm, J. P. Morgan & Co., of $4,000,000 in bonds of the International Mercantile Marine. It was a poor investment. It was deemed unwise to make known to the insurance departments and to present and prospective policy-holders the fact that so large an investment in these unfortunate securities was held by his company (and doubtless also how much they had depreciated in market value).

Perkins, the vice-president of the New York Life company, and at the same time a member of J. P. Morgan & Co., goes through the form on December 31, 1903, of selling $800,000 of these bonds to his firm at par, and then on January 2, 1904, re-transferring the same to the insurance company at par and interest. This was done in order that the officers of the company might under oath present to the insurance departments of the several States and countries an official statement which would show that the insurance company did not at the close of the year 1903 hold as many of these bonds as was the fact, and that the value of those held was par (which was not the fact).

Again, Perkins confesses that in order to prevent the company's exclusion from Prussia by reason of holding among its investments a large amount of stocks, entries were made in the books of account showing a sale of these stocks. The fact is that the stocks were not actually sold, but that their ownership was concealed; and that in order to account on the books for the proceeds of this fake sale, two minor employees of the company — one of them a colored messenger with a salary of $600 per year — were made to give their notes for $3,357,000 with the stock as collateral; and the notes were then represented among the assets. The original purpose of this elaborate system of fraud may have been merely to deceive the Prussian government; but with a degree of thrift rare in the management of these companies, it was used also to deceive our own insurance commissioners and the policy-holders. The New York Life had the effrontery up to the time of Perkins's examination to declare in extensive advertising that it held no stocks whatever.

In the case of common criminals flight is accepted as confession of guilt. With financiers and business men falsification of books has hitherto been considered the strongest evidence of guilt. Yet the falsification of the books of these companies has been a persistent practice.

Secret ledgers have been opened in which were entered questionable investments and more questionable expenditures. Hundreds of thousands spent "for legislative purposes" were charged up in real estate accounts. So elaborate has been the system of fraudulent entries that after months of investigation the particular form of rascality embodied in the Equitable's $685,000 Mercantile Trust Company, so-called "yellow-dog," account has not yet been detected.

The degree of guilt involved in such transactions will be appreciated only when one remembers that the life insurance business beyond all other in the world rests upon confidence — confidence that in the remote, indefinite future the present sacrifice of the policy-holder will bring protection to widow and children.

INEFFICIENCY IN MANAGEMENT

But the management of these companies has been not only selfish and dishonest; it has also been singularly inefficient; and it is by this inefficiency that the policy-holders have actually suffered most. The losses of policy-holders through exorbitant salaries and syndicate operations, though large in the aggregate, are small as compared with the loss from bad management.

The test of success in the life insurance business is of course to furnish insurance of absolute safety at the minimum cost. The size of a life insurance company is no evidence of success. It is evidence of energy; it is evidence of business skill; but the writing by the Mutual Life of $1,578,931,833 of insurance and the control of $442,061,529 in assets is, in itself, no more evidence of success as an insurance company than the display of a $12,000 rug in the office of its president. In life insurance, success is proved by a small pro rata expense account, a large percentage of return upon absolutely safe investments and a small per cent of lapsed and surrendered policies.

Now what is the record of the three largest life insurance companies of the world in this respect? Exclusive of taxes and fees, the percentage of expense to total premium income for 1904 was this:

New York Life, 22.73 per cent.

Equitable, 22.78 per cent.

Mutual Life, 24.65 per cent.

These expense percentages are appalling; and yet the companies which, besides issuing ordinary life policies, make a specialty of insuring the workingmen show an even greater percentage of expense to all premium receipts, namely:

Metropolitan Life, 37.09 per cent.

Prudential, 37.28 per cent.

This Prudential Company, which advertises itself as the Rock of Gibraltar, takes for its officers and other management expenses on the average of all business 37.28 cents for every dollar which the policy-holders deposit with it. On the industrial business, the working-man's insurance, the percentage taken is even larger. In addition, the company pays to stockholders in dividends each year an equivalent of 219.78 per cent on the cash paid into the company on the capital stock.

SAVINGS BANKS BY CONTRAST

Compare these huge life insurance companies' charges for managing savings with the cost of running the Massachusetts savings banks. There are in Massachusetts 188 savings banks under the management of probably about 3,000 different individuals acting as trustees without compensation. At the close of the financial year, October 31, 1904, these banks held assets aggregating $674,644,990.17, more than half the aggregate held by the three largest life insurance companies of the world. There had been deposited in these 188 savings banks during the year ending October 31, 1904, $105,466,-

148.68, an amount exceeding half the aggregate of the year's premiums of these three companies ($206,132,511.44). The aggregate expense of taking care of the business of these 188 savings banks for the year 1904 was $1,546,904.44, or less than one-thirtieth of the aggregate expense of these three insurance companies ($48,106,-809.00) for the year.

To manage the 188 Massachusetts savings banks cost 23-100 of one per cent of the average assets held during the year, or but 1.46 per cent of the year's deposits. To manage the three large life insurance companies cost 4.03 per cent of their aggregate average assets and 23.33 per cent of the year's premium income. That is, the pro rata cost of conducting the insurance business and taking care of the savings invested in these three insurance companies was *seventeen times* as great as the expense of caring for savings invested in our 188 savings banks.

Compare now the service rendered by these two classes of savings institutions. The high-priced insurance managers with their banking and trust company adjuncts and high finance directorates earned for their three companies during the year 1904 the following gross return on investments:

New York Life . . . . . 4.14 per cent.
Equitable . . . . 4.22   "
Mutual Life . . . . . . 4.24   "
_____
Average . . . . 4.20   "

The faithful treasurers of the 188 modest Massachusetts savings banks, supervised mainly by obscure but conscientious citizens, earned during the year ending October 31, 1904, 4.40 per cent on the average assets. The return earned by our savings banks is thus five per cent greater than that of the three insurance companies, and a comparison of net returns is even more favorable to the savings banks. I do not say that the income returns of the great companies manned by the great financiers was unreasonably low, but merely that the small banks with their low salaried officers earned more.

LOSS THROUGH LAPSED POLICIES

The average rate of dividends actually paid or credited to the depositors in our savings banks for the year ending October 31, 1904, was 3.75 per cent with interest compounded semi-annually, and in 1904 no depositor in a Massachusetts savings bank lost a dollar of the principal deposited. On the other hand, the practice of

the insurance companies in relation to forfeiture
and surrender of policies has resulted in a large
percentage of the policy-holders losing a great
part of all they had paid in premiums.

The whole structure of life insurance rests
upon this postulate: while the duration of life
of any individual is uncertain, the average duration of the lives of a large number is certain.
You cannot tell how long any one man of say
twenty-five years will live, but you can say
with certainty that the average age which any
thousand men of twenty-five years now living in
this country will attain is 63.81 years, and that
on the average they will die three and one-half
years later than another thousand who are
thirty years old. If each of these men wanted
$1,000 insurance payable at death — the an-
nual premium for each — (aside from the expense of management) is that sum, which, invested and compounded at the rate which it is
assumed the investment will pay (now taken as
low as 3½ per cent or 3 per cent), will at the
end of 38.81 years yield $1,000. Now among
these 1,000 persons the number of deaths increases each year. But under the level premium system practised by the legal reserve
companies, the premium is always the same;
that is, in the earlier years the insured pays not

only a premium commensurate with the risk of the year, but something on account of the greater risk of future years. For instance, a man at twenty-five pays a premium about twice that which represents the risk of his dying in that year.

Now, a life insurance policy by its terms is usually forfeited unless full premiums are paid for the first three years. Forfeited policies are termed "lapsed" policies. The lapse of a policy results in total loss to the insured of his premium, except for the protection temporarily enjoyed. The voluntary surrender of a policy after three full years' premiums are paid results in a loss of part of the premiums paid — because the companies pay on surrender only a fraction of its actual legal reserve value (*e. g.*, in 1904 the Mutual Life paid on surrender only 63.15 per cent of such value). Experience, especially in these large companies, shows that the mortality of life insurance policies is very much greater than the mortality among policy-holders. The life of an ordinary life policy is short, not because life is short, but because most policies do not come to their natural termination. Thus, in the year 1904 the policies in the Mutual Life which came to a natural termination by death, maturity or expiry aggregated only 9,169 in number and $28,278,464 in amount insured; while 7,011 policies aggregating $16,896,941 were surrendered, and 33,215 policies aggregating $74,909,054 lapsed.

Among the companies which make a specialty of insuring workingmen, the mortality of the policies is very much greater. In 1904, 116,894 of the Metropolitan Company's industrial policies terminated by death and expiry; but 1,223,832 terminated by lapse and 61,220 by surrender; that is, only one policy in twelve came to a natural end. In the Prudential Company the condition was even worse. There 82,963 terminated by death and expiry; 945,-640 by lapse, and 45,361 by surrender; that is, only one policy in thirteen came to a natural end.

WHY POLICIES LAPSE

People who take out fire insurance policies generally continue the insurance, although a fire policy could be dropped after the term without the insured losing anything, since the insured has had his full protection. But in life insurance, where a large premium is paid in early years on account of the greater mortality of later years, the policy-holder who allows his policy to lapse loses the reserve which had accumulated for him. What is the explanation of this huge mortality in life insurance policies? It can be only this: men are induced to take out life insurance by misrepresentation, or by promises which are not realized; and the extravagant conduct of the business renders the cost of the life insurance so great that the insured cannot continue to carry it.

THE WASTE IN SOLICITING

Consider how great this expense of solicitation is. In the year 1904 the New York Life spent in agents' commissions 11.62 per cent of all premiums received; the Equitable, 11.81 per cent; the Mutual Life of New York, 13.57 per cent; the Metropolitan, 15.01 per cent; and the Prudential, 18.98 per cent. Note that this is the average percentage paid for commissions on all policies, old and new. The percentage on new business is of course much greater. The Mutual Life paid in 1904 for commissions on new business $6,691,016.56 out of premiums aggregating $14,676,651.60, or 45.58 per cent of the year's premiums on new business. Yet those figures present only a part of the expense of solicitation. There is, in the next place, all the advertising. For that the Mutual paid in 1904 the greater part of the amount charged to "advertising, printing and postage," which

amounts to $1,134,833.76, or 7.73 per cent of
the year's premium receipts from new business;
and besides this, there is all the office and inspection expense directly entailed by this extensive solicitation. The extent to which solicitation is carried may be inferred from the fact,
that in the year 1904 the Equitable, the Mutual Life and the New York Life actually wrote
102,314 policies carrying an aggregate insurance of $244,862,421, which were not even
taken. That is, the applicant did not pay the
first premium. He was brought "to water,"
but could not be made "to drink." The aggregate expense of solicitation in these three
companies must approximate sixteen per cent
of all premium receipts. When it is borne in
mind how small a part of the policies come to
the natural end of fruition to the policy-holder,
and how great consequently is the loss to the
policy-holder from lapsed and surrendered policies, the extent of the economic waste resulting
from solicitation as practised will be realized.

SAVING THAT IS LOSING

Life insurance is but a method of saving. The
savings banks manage the funds until such time
as they shall be demanded by the depositor —
the insurance company ordinarily until the de-

positor's death.   The savings bank pays back to
the depositor his deposit with interest less the
necessary expense of management.   The insurance company in theory does the same.   The
difference is merely that the savings bank undertakes to repay to each individual depositor
the whole of his deposit with interest; while the
insurance company undertakes to pay to those
who do not reach the average age more than
they have deposited (including interest), and to
those who exceed the average age less than they
deposited (including interest).

How many wage-earners would insure in
these companies if they were told that for every
dollar they pay, forty cents will go to the stockholders', officers' and agents' salaries, or for
other running expenses?   How many wage-earners would assume the burden of premiums if
they knew that there is but one chance in
twelve that they will carry their policies to
maturity?

How idle is the boast sometimes made by
these companies that they have returned to the
policy-holder the whole of his premiums.   It is
as if the savings bank should boast of returning to the depositor all of his deposit but without any interest.   Such practically is what the
Equitable, the New York Life and the Mutual

Life do to-day. The average expense of the three companies, exclusive of taxes and fees, was 4.03 per cent of their aggregate assets, while the average of the return of the three companies on investments was 4.20 per cent. It means in plain English that the company takes as compensation for the care of the policy-holder's money all that that money earns. Such were the terms on which, during the troubled times of the Napoleonic wars, the Duke of Hesse is said to have intrusted his money to Meyer Amschel Rothschild, and to have laid the foundation for what, at least until recently, was the world's greatest fortune.

CAUSES OF ABUSES GENERAL

I have referred specifically to only five of the ninety principal American legal reserve companies, five which are closely allied with Wall Street, which on January 1, 1905, held 56.89 per cent of the aggregate assets, and which during the year 1904 wrote 67.42 per cent of all the life insurance written by the ninety companies. Of the remaining eighty-five, some are doubtless managed far less efficiently and quite as dishonestly as any of the leaders; many are, no doubt, managed with scrupulous honesty, and some with reasonable and comparatively great economy; but the methods of conducting the business, particularly of soliciting new business, adopted by the leaders, is to a greater or less extent, and perhaps necessarily, followed by the others at the present time. The existing evils are not to be explained by the presence in office of dishonest or selfish men. The causes which produce these rank abuses are general in their operation. The flagrant dishonesty and selfishness of the managers of the three leading New York companies are the result, not the cause, of the abuses. Men of character may for a time protect other companies in large part from like abuses, but the main cause of the evils disclosed lies in the system, rather than in the men.

It is obvious that the American people whose attention has once been directed to these abuses will not suffer them to continue without some attempt at a remedy. What are the remedies proposed?

FEDERAL SUPERVISION NO REMEDY

The one most prominently mentioned is Federal supervision. Under the decisions rendered by the Supreme Court of the United States, an act providing for Federal supervision would appear to be clearly unconstitutional. But it is apparently believed that the Supreme Court can be induced to reverse itself. Senator Dryden introduced on February 27, 1905, the bill known as No. 7277, to which attention is invited.

Note the provisions by which this bill seeks to put an end to the intolerable abuses which have been disclosed. An insurance company authorized to do business in the State where organized may, by filing a copy of its charter and a financial statement and depositing $100,-000 in securities with the treasurer of the United States, secure a United States license, which will entitle it to do business in any State unless and until the license is revoked by the Federal superintendent for failure to pay a judgment, or because the company is deemed by him unsafe. The bill omits very many of the provisions which, for instance in Massachusetts, have been inserted for the protection of the policyholder; it adds not a single one by which he may be better protected.

But even if the Federal law contained all the provisions of the best of the State laws, will the insured gain or lose by substituting the supervision of one man at Washington for the supervision of the several States? Assistant Attorney-General Nash of Massachusetts, in his able argument against Federal supervision, has truly said:

"The wisdom, discretion and honesty composite in fifty States and Territories are more to be valued than the excellences of one person appointed at Washington. State supervision is good or bad, according to the merits of the best of the commissioners. Federal supervision must be good or bad, according to the qualities of one man who is unchecked by the work of co-ordinate officials."

The sole effect of a Federal law would be — the purpose of the Dryden bill may have been — to free the companies from the careful scrutiny of the commissioners of some of the States. It seeks to rob the State even of the right to protect its own citizens from the legalized robbery to which present insurance measures subject the citizens, for by the terms of the bill a Federal license would secure the right to do business within the borders of the State, regardless of the State prohibitions, free from the State's protective regulations. With a frankness which is unusual, and an effrontery which is common — among the insurance magnates — this bill is introduced in the Senate by John F. Dryden, the president of the Prudential Life Insurance Company, the company which pays to stockholders annual dividends equivalent to 219.78 per cent for each dollar paid in on the stock; the company which devotes itself mainly to insuring the workingmen at an expense of over 37.28 cents on every dollar of premiums paid; the company which, in 1904, made the worst record of lapsed and surrendered industrial policies.

The Prudential Life Insurance Company has a special reason for desiring to avoid State supervision. Three years ago the Massachusetts insurance commissioner insisted that the policy-holders must be protected from the scandalous financial relations between the Prudential Company and its allied Fidelity Trust Company — from schemes as dangerous to the interest of the insured as any laid bare by the investigations of the Equitable, the New York Life and the Mutual Life.

Federal supervision is also advocated by Mr. James M. Beck (formerly Assistant Attorney-General of the United States), the counsel for the Mutual Life Insurance Company, and his main argument against State supervision appears to be that the companies pay, in the aggregate, for fees and taxes in the several States $10,000,000, which he says is twice as much as is necessary to cover the expense of proper supervision. Ten million dollars is a large sum in itself, but a very small one compared with the aggregate assets or the aggregate expense of management. Mr. Beck's company paid in 1904 $1,138,663 in taxes and fees. Its management expenses were $15,517,520, or nearly fourteen times as much. Our Massachusetts savings banks paid in the year ending October 31, 1904, $1,627,794.46 in taxes to this Commonwealth; that is, $80,890.02 more than their whole expense of management, which was $1,546,904.44.

Doubtless the insurance departments of some States are subjects for just criticism. In many of the States the department is inefficient, in some doubtless corrupt. But is there anything in our experience of Federal supervision of other departments of business which should lead us to assume that it will, in the long run, be freer from grounds of criticism or on the whole more efficient than the best insurance department of any of the States? For it must be remembered that an efficient supervision by the department of any State will in effect protect all the policy-holders of the company wherever they may reside. Federal supervision would serve only to centralize still further the power of our Government and perhaps to increase still further the power of the corporations. Supervision alone — whether State or Federal — will not suffice to correct existing abuses in the life insurance business.

FUNDAMENTAL CHANGES NECESSARY

In order to get rid of the abuses, the measures to be applied must be radical and comprehensive. The changes must be fundamental. They are, in my opinion, these:

Insurance a Method of Saving

First. The recognition of the true nature of the life insurance business; namely, that its sole province is to manage temporarily with absolute safety and at a minimum cost the savings of the people deposited to make appropriate provision in case of death, and that since its province is mainly to aid persons of small means, it should be conducted as a beneficent, not as a money-making, institution.

Abolish the Blind Pool

Second. The issuance of deferred dividend policies should be discontinued. The legitimate business of a life insurance company is to insure the life of the individual and to issue life annuities. It should not be used as an investment company or as a means of gambling on the misfortunes of others. The deferred dividend policy with its semi-tontine provision is open to these objections and to others.

The premium in life insurance is ordinarily computed on a higher death rate than actually prevails, and a lower return upon investment than is actually earned. The profits from these and other sources, unless consumed by excessive expenses or accumulated as surplus, are commonly payable as dividends to the policy-holder either in cash or in reduction of future premiums. Under the deferred semi-tontine dividend policy the dividends are not paid over annually to each policy-holder, but are accumulated for long periods and the accumulated funds distributed, so far as paid out at all, among the surviving policy-holders of a particular class.

The dividends thus accumulated form an appreciable part of the huge funds controlled by the companies. Thus of the $442,061,529.16 assets held on January 1, 1905, by the Mutual Life, $71,539,311.70 consisted of what is called "contingent guaranty fund" and what is really deferred dividends. Of the $412,438,-381 of the assets of the Equitable, it held $63,800,000, which it included under the term "surplus," but which was in fact deferred dividends. The retention of these funds increases unnecessarily the control of quick capital incident to a large business. It promotes also other evils. It tends to extravagance and inefficient management, because it removes the protection which flows from the annual accounting. The annual dividend, the best practical test of the efficiency of the management, is thereby denied to the policy-holders.

The managers control as a "blind pool" this huge fund not required as an insurance reserve. They may with impunity and without discovery make inroads upon it to cover up extravagance, dishonesty, or the results of inefficient management.

Abolish Lavish Commissions

Third. Lavish payments for solicitors' and agents' commissions and for advertising devices should be discontinued. Such practices, common among the promoters of mining enterprises and of patents, have no place in the business of life insurance. Savings banks have no solicitors. The life-insuring habit is well established. The three million people in Massachusetts hold in the thirty-three legal reserve companies doing business in the Commonwealth

1,337,795 life insurance policies, and have only 1,766,614 deposit accounts in our savings banks. The people of the whole United States hold one such policy for every four persons. Undoubtedly many a man has been led by the solicitor's persistence and eloquence to make a thrifty provision for his family. No doubt, also, the savings bank deposits would be swelled by similar exhortation. But can such missionary work be justified at an expense of twelve to twenty per cent of all premiums paid, when the record of lapsed policies shows that the conversion to that thrift is but temporary? In the year 1903 the Metropolitan wrote 1,788,828 industrial policies; in the year 1904 1,223,832 of its industrial policies lapsed. In the year 1903 the Prudential Company wrote 1,468,230 industrial policies; in the year 1904, 945,640 of its industrial policies lapsed. No one should be induced to take out a policy when the burden is greater than he can carry, or if for other reasons it is not for his interest to do so. The intelligent agent with the knowledge and a recognition of the proper function of the life insurance business, and receiving a modest compensation, has still an economic justification. Many men need the impetus to thrift, since wisdom often lags far in the rear of intelligence; but as the business is now conducted, money paid by the insured as a result of solicitation is in large part wasted. The existing abuse is not that the solicitor earns too much, but that his occupation as pursued is economically unjustified.

No Forfeiture of Policies

Fourth. The forfeiture of policies should be prohibited. Under the level premium system everyone pays each year more than is required for the protection of the single year. He pays something on account of future years. That something ought in every case to be preserved for the insured. The excuse offered by the companies for lapsing is the great initial expense of writing insurance, and that arises mainly from the extravagant commissions paid to agents and for lavish advertising. With the suggested change of method in soliciting, no extraordinary expense would be involved in writing insurance except the fee for medical examination, and that should be paid by the applicant as an initiation fee. The insured should know when he enters upon the investment what the initial cost is.

Standard Forms of Policies

Fifth. Standard forms of policy should be prescribed by law. This would go far toward preventing deception. By simplifying and standardizing the contracts, in connection with compulsory annual dividends, the insured would be enabled to compare results in the several companies. To-day such a comparison is practically impossible. The Equitable has outstanding at least 224 different forms of policy; the New York Life, 316; the Mutual Life, 220. Standardizing policies would also much reduce the work (and hence the expense) of the business.

Restrict Investments

Sixth. The investment of the company's funds should be surrounded by safeguards similar to those adopted in the case of savings banks. This would secure safety. This would also go far in preventing the use of funds in speculative enterprises, or to advance private interests, and greatly limit the possibility of the companies engaging in syndicate operations. Investments should not be made in the securities of corporations in which any executive officer or member of the investment committee of the insurance company is interested.

Treasury Safeguards

Seventh. Further to protect the funds of the companies and to prevent their being used directly or indirectly to advance the private or other interests of officers, provision should be made to prohibit the executive officers from engaging in any other business or holding office in any other business corporations. Treasury safeguards also should be adopted to prevent payments without properly authorized warrants.

Accounting and Publicity

Eighth. Methods of accounting should be introduced which would compel the entry of all transactions in a single prescribed set of books, and the submission to the directors at all meetings of reports showing in detail the condition and the operations of the company. In such reports the cost of every department of the business and every kind of business transacted should be clearly determined and disclosed, and likewise the condition, character and result of each investment. Publicity as to the policyholders also is essential to insure the proper conduct of the business by officers and directors.

Directors who Direct

Ninth. The board of directors must be composed of men who recognize the proper function of life insurance companies, and who, like the trustees of our savings banks, recognize the sacred trust involved in their control; men who are willing to give to the companies the time and attention required for the proper performance of a director's duty; men who, having the sole responsibility for the management of the company, will not delegate to the executive officers or committees powers which the board alone should exercise.

Such comprehensive and fundamental changes must be made if existing abuses are to be eradicated; but even they will not prove effective to protect the insured and the community unless in addition:

Limit the Size of Companies

Tenth. A limit must be placed upon the size of the company. A company may, of course, be too small to be a safe or an efficient and economical unit; but it is clearly in the interest of the insured that the company be not allowed to expand beyond the point of greatest efficiency. It is clearly in the interest of the whole people that it be not allowed to expand beyond the point of danger arising from concentration of quick capital in the hands of a few individuals. The constitutional right to so limit the size of insurance companies is undisputed.

Throughout the early years of our history the danger inherent in corporate control was so well understood that in every State limits were placed upon the amount of the authorized capital of corporations of various kinds. The fear of the power of large banking and industrial combinations was then general. Under influences, not always creditable, and under the leadership of New Jersey, that limit upon the amount of capital of corporations has been in many States removed. Now corporations with huge capital are allowed to exist almost everywhere for almost any purpose. Having created them we try ineffectually to check their operations by anti-trust laws. We have tolerated these monster manufacturing and mining companies and the great railroad corporations mainly because it is believed that somehow, through consolidation, the public may be better served. But whatever may be true in other fields of business, it has been proved beyond doubt that in life insurance mere increase in size does not tend to lessen cost of management or to increase returns from investment; that the largest companies are unable to serve the public as well as smaller institutions. It has also been shown conclusively that many of the abuses in the life insurance business, now disclosed, result directly from the size of the companies. Man has not kept pace in growth with his works. Even the executives of the "Big Three" have admitted their inability adequately to supervise their companies. Perkins and other witnesses have sought to excuse illegitimate syndicate transactions and speculative underwritings by the necessities of investing the huge sums pouring into the large companies. On the other hand, the investigation has also made clear that these large insurance companies through the power which inheres in the control of quick capital expose the community to dangers which no other kind of corporation presents to so great an extent.

To eradicate abuses — to protect the community — therefore, it is essential that the insuring unit be kept relatively small. You must limit the amount of premiums which it may receive, and the assets which it may hold — as well as the scope and methods of the business.

These in general are the remedies which in my opinion must be adopted to avoid the abuses incident to the life insurance business as now conducted.

THE INEVITABLE ALTERNATIVE

What is the alternative? Not the discontinuance or substantial reduction of life insurance; for life insurance has become a prime necessity. Not the continuance of the present abuses; for the outraged and enlightened public opinion will no longer tolerate them. If our people cannot secure life insurance at a proper cost and through private agencies which deal fairly with them, or if they cannot procure it through private agencies except at the price of erecting financial monsters which dominate the business world and corrupt our political institutions, they will discard the private agency and resort to State insurance.

Despite your or my protest, the extension of government activity into fields now occupied by private business is urged on every side. Of all services which the community requires, there is none in which the State could more easily engage than that of insuring the lives of its citizens. Stripped of the mysteries with which it has been surrounded, and the misleading devices by which it has been permeated, the business of life insurance is one of extraordinary simplicity. To conduct it successfully requires neither genius nor initiative, and if pursued by the State does not even call for the exercise of any high degree of business judgment. The sole requisites would be honesty, accuracy, persistence and economy.

The business of life insurance, which the companies now make so incomprehensible to the insured, consists properly only of three elements:

1. The initial medical examination.

2. The calculation of the so-called net premium or insurance and mortality reserve.

3. The investment of funds.

The first is the province of the physician; the second a mere matter of arithmetic worked out by the actuary and now actually performed in large part also by our insurance departments as a necessary incident of their supervision; the third, the proper investment of funds, would ordinarily require a high degree of judgment. But if the business were conducted by the State, the proper investment of funds would not, at least in Massachusetts, present any difficulty. The State and municipal loans would take up all insurance reserve. The net indebtedness of the Commonwealth on December 31, 1904, was $74,335,130.12, that of our cities and

towns $141,658,601. This aggregate of $215,-
993,731.11 presents a fund far greater than is
required as the legal reserve for all the policies
now outstanding in this Commonwealth. The
net value of all outstanding legal reserve life
insurance in Massachusetts on January 1, 1905,
was only $122,727,918. The aggregate pre-
miums paid in Massachusetts during the three
years ending January 1, 1905, to the thirty-
three old line companies was $79,033,991; but
the increase during those years of legal reserve
requirement was only $23,122,089. The in-
crease of the net State debt and of the gross
municipal debt during those years aggregated
$34,798,132.74. If the State had done this life
insurance business, the three years' increase of
legal reserve would not have sufficed to meet the
increased borrowings of the State and the mu-
nicipalities. In Massachusetts at least, a safe
investment for our insurance funds would thus
be assured.

The net return from such investment of the
funds by the State would compare not unfavorably with that now received by the leading
insurance companies. It is true that the interest
return on Massachusetts State and municipal
bonds is less than the present average return
of the life insurance companies on investments;

but that return in case of State insurance would
be net.   There would, as to the reserve funds, be
no expense of management.   Furthermore, the
investment return of the insurance companies
is being almost steadily reduced, and the insurance reserve on new business is being calculated
on the basis of three and a half or three per
cent, which is as low as the average return on
State and municipal bonds.

STATE INSURANCE UNDESIRABLE

In my opinion the extension of the functions
of the State to life insurance is at the present
time highly undesirable.   Our Government does
not yet grapple successfully with the duties
which it has assumed, and should not extend
its operations at least until it does.   But whatever and however strong our conviction against
the extension of governmental functions may
be, we shall inevitably be swept farther toward
socialism unless we can curb the excesses of our
financial magnates.   The talk of the agitator
alone does not advance socialism a step; but
the formation of great trusts — the huge railroad consolidations — the insurance "racers"
with the attendant rapacity or the dishonesty
of their potent managers, and their frequent
corruption of councils and legislatures is hasten-

ing us almost irresistibly into socialistic measures. The great captains of industry and of finance, who profess the greatest horror of the extension of governmental functions, are the chief makers of socialism. Socialistic thinkers smile approvingly at the operations of Morgan, Perkins and Rockefeller, and of the Hydes, McCalls and McCurdys. They see approaching the glad day when monopoly shall have brought all industry and finance under a single head, so that with the cutting of a single neck, as Nero vainly wished for his Christian subjects, destruction of the enemy may be accomplished. Our great trust-building, trust-abusing capitalists have in their selfish shortsightedness become the makers of socialism, proclaiming by their acts, like the nobles of France, "After us, the Deluge!"

SAVINGS BANK INSURANCE[1]

THE average expectancy of life in the United States of a man 21 years old is, according to Meech's Table of Mortality, 40.25 years. In other words, take any large number of men who are 21 years old, and the average age which they will reach is 61¼ years.[2]

If a man, beginning with his 21st birthday, pays throughout life 50 cents a week into Massachusetts savings banks, and allows these deposits to accumulate for his family, the survivors will, in case of his death at this average age of 61¼ years, inherit $2,265.90 if an interest rate of 3½ per cent a year is maintained.[3]

If this same man should, beginning at age 21, pay throughout his life the 50 cents a week to the Prudential[4] Insurance Company as premiums on a so-called "industrial" life policy

---

[1] Published in "Collier's Weekly," September 15, 1906.

[2] According to the American Experience Table of Mortality, the expectancy is 41.53 years; according to Dr. Farr's General English Experience Table No. 3, it is 38.80 years.

[3] The average interest rate paid by the Massachusetts savings banks during the ten years ending October 31, 1905, was 3.83 per cent. The lowest average rate of all these banks in any one year (1903) was 3.709 per cent.

[4] The result in other industrial life insurance companies would be substantially the same.

for the benefit of his family, the survivors would
be legally entitled to receive, upon his death
at the age of 61¼ years, only $820.[1]

If this same man, having made his weekly deposit in a savings bank for 20 years, should then
conclude to discontinue his weekly payments
and withdraw the money for his own benefit, he
would receive $746.20. If, on the other hand,
having made for 20 years such weekly payments to the Prudential Insurance Company,
he should then conclude to discontinue payments and surrender his policy, he would be
legally entitled to receive only $165.

So widely different is the probable result to
the workingman if he selects the one or the
other of the two classes of savings investment
which are open to him; and yet life insurance
is but a method of saving. The savings banks
manage the aggregate funds made up of many
small deposits until such time as they shall be
demanded by the depositor; the insurance
company, ordinarily until the depositor's death.
The savings bank pays back to the depositor
his deposit with interest less the necessary expense of management. The insurance company in theory does the same, the difference

---

[1] The payment to be made by the insurance company would be
increased by small amounts from time to time paid by way of benefits or dividends if any are declared.

being merely that the savings bank undertakes to repay to each individual depositor the whole of his deposit with interest; while the insurance company undertakes to pay to each member of a class the average amount (regarding the chances of life and death), so that those who do not reach the average age get more than they have deposited (including interest), and those who exceed the average age less than they deposited (including interest). The fundamental object of both savings and life insurance institutions is the safe and profitable investment and care, at a minimum of expense, of funds contributed from time to time in small amounts. To attain this end, the essential qualities on the part of the management of both classes of institutions are good judgment, honesty, economy and accuracy.

Why, then, does the workingmen's investment in industrial insurance prove relatively so disastrous?

What Industrial Insurance is

Industrial insurance is simply life insurance in small amounts of the kind commonly taken by the wage-earner. In the United States the policies average now about $140. They serve mainly to provide funds to meet the wage-earner's heavy expenses of a last illness and a decent burial. They are considered a prime necessity among the working people, so that of the 20,936,565 level premium life insurance policies outstanding in the ninety American companies on January 1, 1905, 15,678,310 were industrial policies.

The peculiar features of industrial as distinguished from ordinary life insurance are: —

(*a*) That the premiums are fixed for all ages at 5 cents or multiples thereof, the variations for different ages being in the amount of insurance so purchased, whereas in ordinary life insurance the variation is in the amount of premium.

(*b*) That the premium is payable weekly, whereas in ordinary life insurance the premium is payable annually, semi-annually or quarterly.

(*c*) That the premium is collected from house to house, whereas in ordinary life insurance the payments of premium are commonly remitted by mail or are made at the office of the company or of its agents.

THE APPALLING WASTE IN INDUSTRIAL INSURANCE

In the United States about 94 per cent of all industrial insurance is furnished by three com-

INDUSTRIAL.— Infantile Table.

Weekly Premium, *Ten Cents.*

BENEFIT PAYABLE IF POLICY HAS BEEN IN FORCE FOR	Age next birthday when policy is issued.							
	2	3	4	5	6	7	8	9
Less than 3 months	$16	$18	$20	$22	$24	$28	$32	$40
More than 3, but less than 6 months	20	22	26	28	32	38	44	56
More than 6, but less than 9 months	24	28	32	36	44	52	70	100
More than 9 months, but less than 1 year	30	34	40	48	58	70	100	150
One year	34	40	48	58	78	110	160	240
Two years	40	48	58	86	120	170	240	
Three "	48	58	94	130	180	240		
Four "	58	102	140	190	240			
Five "	110	150	200	240				
Six "	160	200	240					
Seven "	200	240						
Eight "	240							

One-half the above amounts will be paid for a weekly premium of five cents. No higher premium than ten cents will be taken.

Table showing the rates charged for baby insurance by the Prudential Insurance Company.
For five cents a week this company will insure a child one year old, paying the parents eight dollars in case of death.

panies, the Metropolitan of New York writing
49 per cent, the Prudential of New Jersey 36 per
cent, and the John Hancock of Massachusetts
9 per cent.   Each company issues also ordinary
life policies.

The Metropolitan (which alone separates in
any published statement the expense of its industrial department from its ordinary life department) discloses that the managing expenses
of its industrial department in the year 1904
(exclusive of real estate taxes, insurance taxes
and departmental fees) was 42.08 per cent of all
premium receipts.   The expense in the John
Hancock is stated to be "about" 40 per cent.
That of the Prudential is probably higher than
either of the other companies.

In the year 1904 the average expense of management of these three companies (including
both the ordinary life and the industrial departments) was 37.21 per cent of all premium
receipts.   Premium receipts of insurance companies correspond to deposits of savings banks.
In the same year the percentage of management expenses to deposits made during the
year of the 188 Massachusetts savings banks
was 1.47 per cent.   In other words, the percentage of expense of management to premium receipts of these insurance companies was twenty-

five times as great as that of the savings banks
to their year's deposits. Yet the percentage of
expense of the industrial department of these
insurance companies alone is even greater than
37.21 per cent of the premium receipts, the companies' percentage of expense being reduced by
reason of the fact that the companies issue also
ordinary life policies. Even the extravagantly
managed Mutual Life, New York Life and
Equitable (which issue only ordinary life policies) took for such managing expenses in 1904,
on the average, only 23.33 per cent of the year's
premium receipts; while the Metropolitan, the
Prudential and the John Hancock (which issued both kinds of policies) took 37.21 per cent.

It is true that the collections of premium by
an insurance company are partly for the purpose
of carrying insurance risk, as well as for that
of investment, while the deposits in a savings
bank are accepted solely for the purpose of investment, but this circumstance does not by
any means wholly destroy the significance of
the foregoing comparisons.

How heavy the burden is which the present
system of industrial life insurance imposes upon
the workingman can, however, be fully appreciated only if we bear in mind the following
facts: —

First — The Double Premium

The premium payable for any given amount of industrial insurance is about double that payable on ordinary life non-participating policies.

Thus, in the Metropolitan, an industrial policy-holder insuring at age 21 would pay 60 cents a week, or in the aggregate 31.20 a year for a $984 policy, while he would pay only $16.55 a year for an ordinary life non-participating $1,000 policy. In the Prudential a man of 40 would pay 50 cents a week, or in the aggregate $26 a year, for a $500 policy, while he would pay only $27.03 for an ordinary life non-participating $1,000 policy.

Second — The Quadruple Expense of Management

The proportion of the premium taken for management expenses in the case of industrial insurance is about twice as great as in the case of ordinary life non-participating policies; and, since the premium also is about twice as great as for an ordinary non-participating life policy of like amount, it follows that the industrial policy-holder pays toward expense of management four times as much as even the present expense charge borne by the ordinary life policy-holder for the same amount of insurance.

Third — The High Lapse Rate

About two-thirds of all industrial policies lapse and are forfeited within three years of the date of issue, the premiums paid thereon proving a total loss to the policy-holder. In the year 1904, 87 per cent of the industrial policies in the Metropolitan, the Prudential and the John Hancock which terminated within the year were forfeited; and only 13 per cent resulted in any payment to the insured.

Of the 2,761,449 industrial insurance policies in these three great companies which terminated by death, surrender and lapse during the year 1904, aggregating in amount $422,633,987, payment was made to insured on only 347,072, or about one-eighth of the policies. In other words, the holders of 2,414,377 policies, with aggregate insurance of $379,708,958, made a total loss of all premiums paid.

The fact that more than 40 per cent of each premium goes to expense of management, when taken alone, fails, therefore, to show how great this industrial insurance waste is. We must remember that the expense is more than 40 per cent of a premium which is double the ordinary

premium.   But even these facts considered together do not fully disclose the waste.   They
indicate only the loss to persisting policy-holders.
We must remember also that those whose policies lapse — a great majority of all who insure
— lose also (except for the temporary protection) the whole 100 per cent of their premiums.

The Causes of this Waste

What are the causes of this appalling waste of
the workingmen's savings?

(A) Not Financial Depravity

Financial depravity is not an important cause.
The recent insurance investigations have, it is
true, disclosed in the Metropolitan and in the
Prudential, as in the Equitable, the New York
Life and the Mutual Life of New York, grave
breaches of trust.   These industrial companies
also have paid exorbitant salaries.   In them
also official position and policy-holders' money
have been used for private profit.   By them
also illegal contributions have been made to
secure legislative favors.   And, in addition, the
stockholders of the Metropolitan and of the
Prudential have, to a degree unknown in ordinary life companies, received unjustifiable dividends.   The capital of the Prudential has been

swelled from $91,000 to $2,000,000 out of the premiums exacted from workingmen, so that now the company, while paying nominally a 10 per cent dividend, in fact pays to its stockholders in dividends each year an equivalent of 219.78 per cent on the cash actually paid in on the capital stock. The capital of the Metropolitan likewise has been swelled out of wage-earners' premiums from $500,000 to $2,000,000, so that now the company, while paying nominally a 7 per cent dividend, in fact pays to stockholders each year an equivalent of 28 per cent on the cash actually paid in on the capital stock. The profitableness of the business to stockholders and officers is further shown by the fact that the Metropolitan, in order to increase its own business and to eliminate competition, bought out, in 1902, a small Kentucky company on terms which netted its stockholders nearly $400 per share for stock on which only $100 had been paid in.

But the amount diverted from policy-holders by financial irregularities, though large in the aggregate, is small as compared with the total of premiums paid. Financial depravity does not explain why in fifteen years the workingmen of Massachusetts have paid $55,285,744 in industrial premiums to these three companies, and received back in all only $19,881,353; that is, 35.96 per cent of the aggregate premiums paid, without interest.[1] The John Hancock appears to have been managed throughout with scrupulous honesty as a mutual company, and yet in the fifteen years ending December 31, 1904, it took from Massachusetts industrial policy-holders in premiums $18,319,730, and paid to them only $5,942,033, or 32.43 per cent, without interest, of the premiums paid.[2]

(B) Not Mere Extravagance

Nor is this fearful waste of workingmen's savings due to mere extravagance in management. The working organization of these companies is said to be admirable; and, aside from a few exorbitant official salaries in the Metropolitan and the Prudential, the employees of the three companies are certainly not overpaid on the average. The Armstrong Report states that, of the 12,000 or 13,000 agents in the Metropolitan, "an enterprising man who devotes his whole time to the business" received an average of $11.64 per week; the 2,112 clerks, an average of $15; the "about 2,700 assistant superintendents,"

---

[1] The figures for the United States are not available, the payments to industrial policy-holders not being separated from those to ordinary policy-holders.

[2] The insurance reserve and some surplus were, of course, accumulated also.

$25 a week; and the "about 350 superinten-
dents," $50; and that the fees paid for each
medical examination and inspection were 50 cents
and 25 cents respectively: that the Prudential
paid to 8,582 agents on the average $14.61 per
week; to 1,751 assistant superintendents, $24.24;
and to 223 superintendents, $95.55. Obviously,
therefore, mere extravagance is not the cause
of this waste of workingmen's savings.

(C) *The System Vicious*

The real cause of these meagre results to the
insured from industrial insurance is not financial depravity or extravagance, but the extraordinary wastefulness necessarily attendant upon
the present system of supplying life insurance
for workingmen.

The principal elements of expense in industrial insurance are:

(1) The initial expense on issue of policies,
taken in connection with the large percentage
of policies lapsed.

(2) The expense of house-to-house collection
of weekly premiums.

(A) THE INITIAL EXPENSE

The average initial expense as figured by the
Metropolitan was, in 1904, $2.07 per policy on

which the average premium was 12 cents weekly. It is probably about the same in other companies. In the John Hancock the initial expense includes the agent's commission at the rate of 48 cents for placing a policy bearing 5 cents weekly premium, and the physician's fee of 50 cents. But the issue of each policy involves besides these specific charges a large pro rata for general expense, the exact amount of which is not supplied by the published accounts. The initial charge, while large in itself as compared with the year's premiums, becomes particularly burdensome to persisting policy-holders by reason of the heavy lapse rate.

"From the most careful accounting made time and again," says the John Hancock, "the weekly premium policies do not square themselves and make good the initial and current expenses and loss and provide for the State requirement of reserve, until at least three full years' premiums have been paid. . . . Not a policy that lapses before at least three full years' premiums have been paid but leaves a greater or less deficiency for the survivors to bear. . . ."

" On the average fully one-half the entrants lapse their policies before the end of the first year and a majority of these within the first quarter, though no policy lapses until four weekly premiums are overdue."

The experience of the John Hancock is, of course, not exceptional. The Metropolitan lapse rate appears to be larger, and that of the Prudential still larger. The Armstrong Committee found that in the Metropolitan, —

"More than one-third of the policies issued do not survive three months, and about one-half are cancelled within a year. In 1903 the company took one week's industrial issue from each month in the year, and followed the issue through a period of twelve months, with the following result:

								Per cent.
Rate of lapses in first	3	months from date of issue				. .	35.40
" "	"	6	"	"	"	"	. .	43.57
" "	"	9	"	"	"	"	. .	48.28
" "	"	12	"	"	"	"	. .	51.46

In 1904 the average time for which premiums were paid on policies which lapsed within one year from issue was 6.05 weeks.

The net result to the Metropolitan Company from each policy so lapsed is as follows: —

Initial cost of policy	$2.07
Cost of carrying policy	.52
	$2.59
Average weekly premiums at 12.004 cents for 6.05 weeks	.726
Net loss to the company (*i. e.*, to the persisting policy-holders)	$1.864
Net loss to the insured (12.004 cents per week for 6.05 weeks)	.726

During the second year (in which about 10 per cent of the policies lapse) and the third year (in which about 5 per cent lapse) the net loss to the company (that is, to the persisting policy-holders) grows gradually less, but that to the insured whose policies lapse grows very much greater. For, while the average net loss to the insured whose policies lapse during the first year is about 73 cents, the average, figured on the same basis, for those whose policies lapse in the second year is approximately $8.88, and the average net loss to those whose policies lapse in the third year is approximately $15.12. In 1904 the Metropolitan wrote 1,829,559 new policies. Applying the above percentages to the business of the Metropolitan for the full years of 1904 and 1905, we find that 941,491 of the 1,829,559 policies written in 1904 must have lapsed within the year 1905, and that the net loss on these lapsed policies aggregated $2,438,-461.68, of which the insured bore $683,522.46, and the persisting policy-holders $1,754,939.22.

(B) The Collection Charge

But besides the deficit due to lapses the persisting policy-holder bears another fearful burden. Even in the honestly managed John Hancock the fee of the collector is 20 per cent of

each week's premium, and this 20 per cent charge
is only a part of the cost of collection. There
is in addition necessarily the large expense of
an elaborate system of superintendence and
accounting. Bear in mind that 20 per cent of
an industrial premium is equal to 40 per cent of
the sum payable as premium for a like amount
of ordinary insurance.

Obviously, therefore, a substantial reduction
of the present cost of industrial insurance is not
possible unless some radical change of system
be introduced whereby the initial expenses, the
cost of premium collection, and the percentage
of lapses is greatly lessened.

THE SACRIFICE OF THE THRIFTY

The supporters of the present system of industrial insurance declare that such a reduction
of expenses and of lapses is impossible. They
insist that the total loss to the insured and the
heavy burden to the policy-holders from lapses,
as well as from the huge cost of premium collection, must all be patiently borne as being the
unavoidable incidents of the beneficent institution of life insurance when applied to the workingman. They declare that the appalling waste
incident to the forfeiture within three years of
two-thirds of all policies written is a sacrifice

essential to the ultimate salvation of the small persisting minority, and that the huge expense involved in the house-to-house collection of weekly premiums is necessary to prevent still more lapses on account of the workingman's alleged lack of thrift.

It may be questioned whether, in view of the heavy expense now attending industrial insurance, the discontinuance of premium payments which yield such slight probability of net returns is not evidence rather of thrift than of thriftlessness. It is surely difficult to justify a system of insurance as to which it may be foretold that, of the millions who are entered each year at a per capita initial expense of $2.07, a majority will not only let their policies lapse within the year, but will on the average pay in premiums only 72 cents. Does not such a record of mortality in policies prove conclusively that most of the entrants had been over-persuaded or misled into taking the insurance? But if, as the companies contend, the discontinuance of premium payments is evidence of thriftlessness, surely the thrifty who persevere should not be compelled to submit to a system which requires such great and largely useless sacrifices in the supposed interest of a small minority.

The thrifty workingman, like people of larger

means, should have the opportunity of obtaining life insurance at more nearly its necessary cost.

THE REMEDY

The sacrifice incident to the present industrial insurance system can be avoided only by providing an institution for insurance which will recognize that its function is not to induce working people to take insurance regardless of whether they really want it or can afford to carry it, but rather to supply insurance upon proper terms to those who do want it and can carry it, — an institution which will recognize that the best method of increasing the demand for life insurance is not eloquent, persistent persuasion, but, as in the case of other necessaries of life, is to furnish a good article at a low price.

THE SAVINGS BANK THE BEST MEDIUM

Massachusetts, in its 189 savings banks, and the other States with savings banks similarly conducted, have institutions which, with a slight enlargement of their powers, can at a minimum of expense fill the great need of life insurance for workingmen.

The only proper elements of the industrial

insurance business not common to the savings bank business are simple, and can be supplied at a minimum of expense in connection with our existing savings banks. They are: —

(a) Fixing the terms on which insurance shall be given.

(b) The initial medical examination.

(c) Verifying the proof of death.

The last involves an inquiry similar in character to that now performed by the clerks of savings banks in the identification of depositors.

The second is the work of a physician, who is available at no greater expense to the savings bank than to the insurance company.

The first is the work of an insurance actuary, who would be equally available to the savings banks as he is to insurance companies, if the former undertook the insurance business. And the present cost of actuarial service can be greatly reduced: first, by limiting the forms of insurance to two or three standard forms of simple policies, uniform throughout the State; and, secondly, by providing for the appointment of a State actuary, who, in connection with the insurance commissioner, shall serve all the savings insurance banks. The work of such an actuary is, indeed, now necessarily performed in large part in each State by the insurance department, as an incident of supervising life insurance companies.

The savings banks could thus enter upon the insurance business under circumstances singularly conducive to extending to the workingman the blessing of safe life insurance at a low cost, because: —

First. The insurance department of savings banks would be managed by experienced trustees and officers who had been trained to recognize that the business of investing the savings of persons of small means is a quasi-public trust which should be conducted as a beneficent and not as a selfish money-making institution.

Second. The insurance department of savings banks would be managed by trustees and officers who in their administration of the savings of persons of small means had already been trained to the practice of the strictest economy.

Third. The insurance business of the savings banks, although kept entirely distinct as a matter of investment and accounting, would be conducted with the same plant and the same officials, without any large increase of clerical force or incidental expense, except such as would be required if the bank's deposits were increased. Until the insurance business attained considerable dimensions, probably the addition of even a single clerk might not be necessary. The business of life insurance could thus be established as an adjunct of a savings bank without incurring that heavy expense which has ordinarily proved such a burden in the establishment of a new insurance company.

If the individual risks were limited at first to, say, $150 on a single life, the business could be begun safely on a purely mutual basis as soon as a few hundred lives were insured, or earlier if a guaranty fund were provided. As the business increased, the limit of single risks could be correspondingly increased, but should probably not exceed $500.

Fourth. The insurance department of savings banks would open with an extensive and potent good will, and with the most favorable conditions for teaching, at slight expense, the value of life insurance. The safety of the institution would be unquestioned. For instance, in Massachusetts the holders of the 1,829,487 savings bank accounts, a number equal to three-fifths of the whole population of the State, would at once become potential policy-holders; and a small amount of advertising would soon suffice to secure a reasonably large business without solicitors.

Fifth. With an insurance clientèle composed

largely of thrifty savings bank depositors, house-to-house collection of premiums could be dispensed with. The more economical monthly payments of premiums could also probably be substituted for weekly payments.

Sixth. A small initiation fee could be charged, as in assessment and fraternal associations, to cover necessary initial expenses of medical examination and issue of policy. This would serve both as a deterrent to the insured against allowing policies to lapse and a protection to persisting policy-holders from unjust burdens which the lapse of policies casts upon them.

Seventh. The safety of savings banks would, of course, be in no way imperilled by extending their functions to life insurance. Life insurance rests upon substantial certainty, differing in this respect radically from fire, accident and other kinds of insurance. As Insurance Commissioner Host, of Wisconsin, said in a recent address: —

"If we take a number of thousand persons of different ages, nothing is more certain in nature than that their natural deaths will occur in a series not differing very widely from that of other thousands of persons under similar circumstances.

"The practical experience of this theory has given to the world the mortality tables upon which life in-

surance premiums are ascertained and the reserves
for the future needs calculated.

"No life insurance company has ever failed which
complied strictly with the law governing the calculation, maintenance, and investment of the legal
reserve. . . ."

The causes of failure in life insurance companies since Elizur Wright established the
science have been excessive expense, unsound
investment, or rapacious or dishonest management. To the risk of these abuses all financial
institutions are necessarily subject, but they
are evils from which our savings banks have
been remarkably free. This practical freedom
of our savings banks from these evils affords a
strong reason for utilizing them to supply the
kindred service of life insurance.

The theoretical risk of a mortality loss in a
single institution greater than that provided
for in the insurance reserve could be absolutely
guarded against, however, by providing a general guaranty fund, to which all savings-insur-
ance banks within a State would make small
pro rata contributions, — a provision similar
to that prevailing in other countries, where all
banks of issue contribute to a common fund
which guarantees all outstanding bank notes.

Eighth. In other respects, also, co-operation

between the several savings insurance banks within a State would doubtless, under appropriate legislation, be adopted; for instance, by providing that each institution could act as an agent for the others to receive and forward premium payments.

Ninth. The law authorizing the establishment of an insurance department in connection with savings banks should, obviously, be permissive merely. No savings bank should be required to extend its functions to industrial insurance until a majority of its trustees are convinced of the wisdom of so doing.

The savings banks are not, however, the only existing class of financial institutions which could be utilized for the purpose of supplying, at a low expense rate, insurance in small amounts under a system requiring frequent premium payments. Co-operative banks, as operated in Massachusetts and in some other States, would, under appropriate regulation, be admirably adapted to supply a part of the required service. The excellent record of these institutions in Massachusetts presents a most encouraging exhibit of the achievements of financial democracy when applied to small units and when operating under a wise system of supervision.

Public attention having at last been directed

to this subject, our workingmen will not long submit to the needless sacrifice of their hard-earned savings, described in the following judgment of the "Armstrong Committee" on the methods of the Metropolitan Company: —

"In fine the industrial department furnishes insurance at twice the normal cost to those least able to pay for it; a large porportion, if not the greater number of the insured, permitting their policies to lapse, receive no money return for their payments. Success is made possible by thorough organization on a large scale and by the employment of an army of underpaid solicitors and clerks; and from margins small in individual cases, but large in the aggregate, enormous profits have been realized upon insignificant investment."

If an opportunity for cheaper life insurance is afforded by means of an extension of the functions of our savings banks, the present industrial insurance companies may be permitted to pursue their efforts at inculcating thrift in accordance with the system which seems to them wise, and their claim that the present huge waste is inevitable will be duly tested.

But if we fail to offer to workingmen some opportunity for cheaper insurance through private or quasi-private institutions, the ever-ready remedy of State insurance is certain to be resorted to soon; and there is no other sphere of business now deemed private upon which the State could so easily and so justifiably enter as that of life insurance.

However great the waste in present life insurance methods, our workingmen will not be induced to abandon life insurance. To them, as to others, life insurance has become a prime need. It must be continued. It should be encouraged. In spite of the disastrous results of this form of savings investment, the industrial insurance business has assumed enormous proportions. On December 31, 1904, the number of industrial life policies outstanding in the three great companies (Metropolitan, Prudential and John Hancock) was 14,731,463, as against a total of only about 5,258,255 ordinary life policies outstanding in the ninety legal reserve companies. The New York Life, with its record of 957,201 policies outstanding, had only one-eighth as many policy-holders as the Metropolitan, one-sixth as many as the Prudential and three-fifths as many as the John Hancock. In the year 1904 alone the Metropolitan, Prudential and John Hancock wrote 3,742,209 industrial policies; that is, more than three times as many as the 90 leading level premium companies wrote of ordinary life policies during that year. In Massachusetts the predominance of industrial policies is even greater than the average. With a population of 3,000,680 there were outstanding December 31, 1904, 1,080,003 industrial policies; that is, one for every three inhabitants, counting men, women and children, and of ordinary life policies only 257,792 were outstanding.

The demand of workingmen for life insurance will continue and will grow; but the yearly tribute of the workingmen to Prudential stockholders of dividends equivalent to 219.78 per cent on the capital actually paid into the company, the yearly waste of millions in lapsed policies, in fruitless solicitation and in needless collections, will cease. The question is merely whether the remedy shall be applied through properly regulated private institutions or whether the State must itself enter upon the business of life insurance.

SUCCESSES OF SAVINGS BANK
LIFE INSURANCE

THE project of the Massachusetts system was first published in *Collier's Weekly*, September 15, 1906. Its main purpose was to eliminate or to mitigate so far as possible, the evils incident to the system of industrial life insurance as then practiced by private companies. The causes of these evils were investigated; and it was proposed to remove them by creating a competitive system upon a new plan.

In 1906 there were outstanding in the United States 17,841,396 industrial life insurance policies, representing $2,453,603,707 of insurance. Three companies, the Metropolitan, the Prudential and the John Hancock, did together 94.3 per cent of this business. The rates and terms to policy-holders of the three companies did not vary materially the one from the others.

Throughout the thirty years of American experience in industrial life insurance prior to September, 1906, there had been substantially no improvement in the position of the policy-

holder. On the contrary, it had rather worsened.
The insured suffered mainly from three evils:

(a) The high premium.

(b) Over-persuasion leading to taking out of
insurance which was bound soon to lapse.

(c) Illiberal and oppressive provisions in the
policies.

During these thirty years the cost of insurance to the policy-holder had gradually increased. In 1887 the rates were on the average
nearly 12 per cent higher than the rates prevailing from 1879 to 1887. In 1896 they were again
increased about 8 per cent on the average over
the rates fixed in 1887; and they remained at
that level until shortly after September, 1906.
Vice-President Haley Fiske of the Metropolitan,
testifying before the Armstrong Committee in
1905, declared that the high expense of industrial
life insurance was unavoidable.

During these thirty years the lapse rate had
not been materially reduced. Of the policies
written in 1903 more than one-third lapsed
within three months and more than one-half
within twelve months from the date of issue.

During these thirty years the policies, instead
of becoming more liberal in their provisions,
had been modified from time to time, so that the
chances of the insured receiving benefits from

the insurance were small. For instance: Until shortly after September, 1906, the policies provided that if death occurred within three months from the date of the policy nothing would be payable under the contract; if death occurred after three months and within the first six months, only one-quarter of the face of the policy would be payable; if death occurred after six months and before the end of twelve months, one-half the face of the policy would be payable. These provisions were much less favorable than those prevailing during the earlier years of industrial life insurance in America.

Furthermore, in 1906 there was no opportunity of getting extended insurance or paid-up insurance until after the end of five years after the date of the policy, and none of getting a cash surrender value at any time. The policies had no loan value.

The Metropolitan Life Insurance Company had been quite fully investigated by the Armstrong Committee in 1905. The officials of the Metropolitan company in testifying before that committee could give no promise of any improvement in the position of the policy-holder; the report of the Armstrong Committee contained no recommendations for remedying the evils disclosed; and the New York remedial legislation of 1906 was so framed as not to apply to industrial insurance.

The discussions incident to the Massachusetts Savings Bank Insurance plan, beginning in September, 1906, the enactment of the legislation on June 26, 1907, and the practical introduction of the system in June, 1908, with the actual and potential competition resulting, have wrought important changes in the rates, methods and practices of the industrial companies which have mitigated in large measure the flagrant abuses at which the reform was aimed, namely:

THE CHANGES WROUGHT

1. The cost of industrial insurance furnished by the Metropolitan and other private companies (expressed in the amount purchased by a given weekly premium) has been repeatedly reduced since September, 1906; so that to-day it is (on the average) about 20 per cent lower than it was then.

2. The methods pursued by the private companies in soliciting industrial insurance have been improved since September, 1906, so that the lapse rate is materially reduced. Thus: Taking the three years 1904, 1905 and 1906 the percentage of lapse of outstanding policies to

the number of policies issued during those years was 65. Taking the three years 1910, 1911 and 1912 the percentage of lapse was only 56. Or, making the comparison on the basis of the amount of insurance: In the three years 1904, 1905 and 1906 the amount of insurance lapsed was 68 per cent of the amount written; whereas in the three years 1910, 1911 and 1912 the percentage of lapses was only 58 per cent of the amount written.

3. The provisions of the insurance policies issued by the private companies have been made more just and liberal. For instance, on January 1, 1907, the amount payable in case of death was increased from nothing, if occurring during the first three months, and one-fourth, if occurring during the second three months, to one-half the face value of the policy if death occurred at any time within the first six months. And the amount payable in case of death during any part of the second six months was increased from one-half to the full face of the policy. Under the changes made January 1, 1907, the premiums, which previously had been payable throughout life, were made to cease at age seventy-five.

4. Paid-up insurance is now granted by the private companies after three years, whereas be-

fore September, 1906, no paid-up insurance was granted until after the end of five years from the date of the policy. It is noteworthy that this change was effected as of January 1, 1907, although Vice-President Haley Fiske had declared before the Armstrong Committee in 1905 that "Any law requiring the issue of paid-up policies in industrial insurance after three years would be most unjust" to the persisting policy-holders.

5. Since September, 1906, the private companies have provided for cash surrender values after the end of ten years, although previously no cash surrender values had been granted.

6. Since September, 1906, the private companies have made their policies incontestable one year after date of issue, whereas theretofore the policies had been incontestable only after two years.

7. Since September, 1906, extended insurance is said to be granted after three years from the date of the policy, whereas none had been granted theretofore.

The improvements made by the private industrial insurance companies as the result of the Massachusetts plan, have of course been extended to their entire business throughout the United States. When it is remembered that the aggregate premium income of the industrial

policies in the United States is now about $115,-
000,000 a year, it seems clear that the industrial
policy-holders throughout the country are to-
day buying their insurance for at least $20,000,-
000 a year less than they would have had to
pay for the same amount of insurance had the
rates prevailing prior to September, 1906, remained in force.

Massachusetts' Gain

The weekly premiums collected by the industrial insurance companies from Massachusetts
wage-earners each year exceed $10,000,000.
The saving to the Massachusetts policy-holders
in the private companies which has resulted
from the competition of its State-aided system is
nearly $2,000,000 a year: while the Common-
wealth's contribution to the expenses of the
system has averaged less than $15,000 a year.
But residents of Massachusetts who availed
themselves of the opportunity which savings
bank insurance affords, have had these further
advantages:

First. The gross rates on the monthly premium savings bank policies in Massachusetts
are on the average about 17 per cent less
than the *now* prevailing rates of the private
industrial companies. The Metropolitan and

Prudential companies, however, issue only non-participating policies, whereas the Massachusetts savings bank policies are participating. The dividends declared on these savings bank policies have been as follows:

	Per Cent.
On policies completing their first anniversary	8⅓
On policies completing their second anniversary . . .	12½
On policies completing their third anniversary	14
On policies completing their fourth anniversary . . .	16⅔
On policies completing their fifth anniversary	20

Therefore the net cost to the insured, for instance, in the fourth year is, on the average, about 32 per cent less, and in the fifth year 35 per cent less than the *present* rates of the private industrial companies.

The policies in one of the private companies, the John Hancock, are participating, but only after five years from the date of issue.

Second. The policies issued by the Massachusetts savings banks are far more liberal even than those *now* written by the private industrial companies. The full face of the policy is payable in case of death at any time after the issue of the policy. Cash surrender value, paid-up insurance and extended insurance are granted at any time after six months from the date of the issue of the policy. The policies have also a loan value after the end of the first year.

Third. A recent investigation of the business of the banks shows that of the policies issued and having twelve months' experience, 25.5 per cent of the number of policies and 26.2 per cent of the amount of insurance are cancelled within a year, whereas in the large industrial companies over 50 per cent of the policies written are cancelled within the first year.

Furthermore the so-called cancellations of the savings insurance banks include all policies surrendered within twelve months, whether by lapse, by death or by surrender for cash. On the bank policies surrendered after six months, $20,336.50 in cash was returned to the policy-holders, and other bank policy-holders also received by way of amounts applied to purchase paid-up insurance $3,924.23. This $24,260.73 would have been entirely lost to the policy-holders had they been insured in the industrial companies.

THE INSURANCE BANKS

On February 28, 1914, the insurance departments of the four savings banks had outstanding 8413 policies, representing $3,316,005 insurance and $29,482 annuities.

Five years after the Massachusetts system was introduced, the banks held an accumulated surplus equal to nearly 10 per cent of the aggregate premium income for the five years, and equal to 14.8 per cent of the aggregate legal policy reserve.

The aggregate premiums collected during these five years were as follows:

Premium income for the first year $25,377.29
Premium income for the second year 58,890.68
Premium income for the third year 76,348.92
Premium income for the fourth year 102,832.27
Premium income for the fifth year 124,205.08

THE EFFECT ON THE BANKS

Four banks have established insurance departments, the third not until August, 1911, and the fourth on July 5, 1912. Fifteen other savings banks and four trust companies have become public agencies for these four banks, and there are also twenty-three other public agencies and about two hundred private agencies. In two banks, the People's Savings Bank of Brockton and the Whitman Savings Bank, the insurance department has been conducted for more than five years. The effect has been to increase markedly the number of their depositors. Massachusetts had, in 1911, 192 savings banks, of which 144 had deposits exceeding $1,000,000. Both the People's Savings Bank of

Brockton and the Whitman Savings Bank were among the smaller banks of that class. The Whitman bank is located in a town of 7,639 inhabitants.

The rate of increase of deposits in these two banks, as compared with the other savings banks in the State, shows the marked effect which the establishment of an insurance department has in stimulating the business of the deposit department. Of the 144 Massachusetts savings banks whose deposits exceeded $1,000,000, these two banks stood among the first five in the rate of increase in deposits for the year ending October 31, 1910, over the previous year; the People's Savings Bank of Brockton standing first and the Whitman Savings Bank, fifth. In the year ending October 31, 1911, these two banks headed this list of Massachusetts savings banks in the rate of increase; the Whitman Savings Bank standing first and the People's Savings Bank second. That the leading position taken in these two years by the Brockton and Whitman banks is due to the insurance department is made more clear by the fact that the other three banks which stood with them among the first five in the year 1910 lost their rank as leaders in the year 1911.

The treasurer of the Whitman bank states:

"I have been unable to find that the Insurance Department has been an injury to the bank in any particular. On the other hand, this department has brought the attention of the public to this institution, with the result that for the past four years our gains have been greater than any savings bank in any other town in Plymouth County.

"As savings banks are organized for the purpose of encouraging thrift and economy, it would seem to me that we have not departed from the original purpose in establishing a life insurance department, which bears a close relationship to savings bank business."

And the treasurer of the People's Savings Bank of Brockton states as follows:

"The writer has been of the opinion from the start that it was a good thing both for the banks and the public, and after observing the practical working of the plan for a period of a little over three years I can say that I am more impressed now than at the beginning.

"Many criticisms were made, as is always the case with anything new, but none of them were well founded and none of the disastrous results predicted have materialized.

"The banks are bigger, better and busier than they were when the insurance departments were opened, and pages could be written setting forth the benefits derived by the policy-holders and beneficiaries.

"Now that there is no longer any doubt of the success of the movement, the banks and the public are voluntarily interesting themselves in the plan.

"The public now come to the bank and apply for insurance and I am sure this will increase as time goes on and will force all critics back to the tall timber."

The establishment of an insurance department is also serving to develop the habit of saving in policy-holders. As to this we have striking evidence in connection with the opening of new deposit accounts at the times when dividends are declared on the policies, and at the times when policies are taken out.

How Bank Insurance is Developed

The business of the savings insurance banks has been developed in large measure through the educational work conducted by the Massachusetts Savings Insurance League. This league was organized on November 26, 1906, by public-spirited citizens of Massachusetts to promote the enactment of the savings bank insurance law. Its work was educational. It undertook to familiarize the people of Massachusetts with the evils incident to the then existing system of industrial life insurance, and to point out the advantages of the Massachusetts plan of savings bank insurance. After the law was enacted the league exerted itself to secure the establishment of insurance departments by the People's

Savings Bank of Brockton, and by the Whitman Savings Bank, and also the establishment of agencies. Since that time it has been engaged in active educational work throughout the Commonwealth. It is largely through the medium of the League that the advantages of the system have been made known to the people.

The League has been instrumental in interesting the large number of manufacturers and others who have established unpaid agencies through which the insurance is written. Its purpose is to bring to the attention of the wage-earners of Massachusetts the importance of making wise provision for the future out of current earnings, either through life insurance or old-age pensions; to endeavor by way of suggestion to encourage them to habits of thrift and foresight; and to acquaint them with the value of savings bank insurance as a means to this end.

THE COMPANIES' CONTENTION

Officials of the private industrial insurance companies point to the relatively small number of policies issued by the Massachusetts insurance banks as evidence that the system has not succeeded. The contrary is true. The initiation of the competitive system was so effective in reforming the most flagrant of the abuses of the industrial companies, that competition with them is necessarily much more difficult than it would have been had the old conditions persisted. And the benefit of these reforms is now enjoyed by nearly every industrial policy-holder in the United States.

It has also been asserted by the Metropolitan Company that while the great improvements in the position of the industrial policy-holder followed the initiation of the Massachusetts plan, they were not the result of the prospective and actual competition of the new system. It is believed that no basis exists for this contention of the company. There was no indication of effort or intention on the part of the industrial insurance companies to improve the situation of the policy-holder until after the Massachusetts campaign was commenced by the article in *Collier's*. On the contrary, the testimony of the Metropolitan's officials before the Armstrong Committee indicated that improvement was believed to be impossible. Furthermore the improvement suddenly made after the discussion incident to the presentation of the Massachusetts plan, and its potential and actual competition are not the only evidence that the Massachusetts plan produced the improvements. More will be found by comparing the changes made by the industrial insurance companies in the provisions of of their policies enumerated above, with the provisions of the policies issued under the Massachusetts system. The reforms introduced by the industrial companies since September, 1906 are clearly due, in the main, to the actual and potential competition of Savings Bank Insurance.

TRUSTS AND EFFICIENCY[1]

LEADERS of the Progressive Party argue that industrial monopolies should be legalized, lest we lose the efficiency of large-scale production and distribution. No argument could be more misleading. The issue of competition *versus* monopoly presents no such alternative as "Shall we have small concerns or large?" "Shall we have ill-equipped plants or well-equipped?"

In the first place, neither the Sherman law nor any of the proposed perfecting amendments (La Follette-Lenroot bill or Stanley bill) contain any prohibition of mere size. Under them a business may *grow* as large as it will or can — without any restriction or without any presumption arising against it. It is only when a monopoly is attempted, or when a business, instead of being allowed to *grow* large, is *made* large by combining competing businesses in restraint of trade, that the Sherman law and the proposed perfecting amendments can have any application. And even then the Sherman

[1] Published in "Collier's Weekly," September 14, 1912.

law and the proposed amendments would not necessarily restrict size. They merely declare that *if there has been such a combination in restraint of trade* the combiners have the burden of showing that it was reasonable, or, in other words, consistent with the public welfare; and that if such a combination controls more than thirty per cent of the country's business it will, in the absence of explanation, be deemed unreasonable.

In the second place, it may safely be asserted that in America there is no line of business in which all or most concerns or plants must be concentrated in order to attain the size of greatest efficiency. For, while a business may be too small to be efficient, efficiency does not grow indefinitely with increasing size. There is in every line of business a unit of greatest efficiency. What the size of that unit is cannot be determined in advance by a general rule. It will vary in different lines of business and with different concerns in the same line. It will vary with the same concern at different times because of different conditions. What the most efficient size is can be learned definitely only by experience. The unit of greatest efficiency is reached when the disadvantages of size counterbalance the advantages. The unit of greatest efficiency is exceeded when the disadvantages of size outweigh the advantages. For a unit of business may be too large to be efficient as well as too small. And in no American industry is monopoly an essential condition of the greatest efficiency.

The history of American trusts makes this clear. That history shows:

First. No conspicuous American trust owes its existence to the desire for increased efficiency. "Expected economies from combination" figure largely in promoters' prospectuses; but they have never been a compelling motive in the formation of any trust. On the contrary, the purpose of combining has often been to curb efficiency or even to preserve inefficiency, thus frustrating the natural law of survival of the fittest.

Second. No conspicuously profitable trust owes its profits largely to superior efficiency. Some trusts have been very efficient, as have some independent concerns; but conspicuous profits have been secured mainly through control of the market — through the power of monopoly to fix prices — through this exercise of the taxing power.

Third. No conspicuous trust has been efficient enough to maintain long, as against the independents, its proportion of the business of the country without continuing to buy up, from time to time, its successful competitors.

These three propositions are also true of most of the lesser trusts. If there is any exception, the explanation will doubtless be found in extraordinary ability on the part of the managers or unusual trade conditions.

And this further proposition may be added:

Fourth. Most of the trusts which did not secure monopolistic positions have failed to show marked success or efficiency, as compared with independent competing concerns.

THE MOTIVES FOR TRUST BUILDING

The first proposition is strikingly illustrated by the history of the Steel Trust. The main purpose in forming that trust was to eliminate from the steel business the most efficient manufacturer the world has ever known — Andrew Carnegie. The huge price paid for his company was merely the 'bribe required to induce him to refrain from exercising his extraordinary ability to make steel cheaply. Carnegie could make and sell steel several dollars a ton cheaper than any other concern. Because his competitors were unable to rise to his remarkable efficiency, his business career was killed; and

the American people were deprived of his ability
— his genius — to produce steel cheaply.   As
the Stanley Investigating Committee found,
the acquisition of the Carnegie Company by the
promoters of the Steel Trust was *"not the
purchase of a mill, but the retirement of a man."*

That finding is amply sustained by the evidence.

The commissioner of the Steel Plate Association, Mr. Temple, testified:

"They had to buy the Carnegie Steel Company.
Mr. Carnegie, with his then plant and his organization and his natural resources, was in a position where
he could dominate the entire situation; and had the
United States Steel Corporation not have been formed
about the time it was — some ten years ago — the
steel business not only of America but of the world
to-day would be dominated by Andrew Carnegie."

George W. Perkins, himself a director of the
Steel Trust, through whose firm (J. P. Morgan
& Co.) the bribe to Carnegie was paid, confirms
Temple's statement:

"The situation was very critical.   If the Steel
Corporation had not been organized, or something
had not been done to correct a very serious condition
at that time, in my judgment by this time Mr. Carnegie would have personally owned the major part
of the steel industry of this country. . . ."

And Herbert Knox Smith, Commissioner of Corporations, after elaborate investigation, declared:

"The conclusion is inevitable, therefore, that the price paid for the Carnegie Company was largely determined by fear on the part of the organizers of the Steel Corporation of the competition of that concern. Mr. Carnegie's name in the steel industry had been long synonymous with aggressive competition, and there can be little doubt that the huge price paid for the Carnegie concern was, in considerable measure, for the specific purpose of eliminating a troublesome competitor, and Mr. Carnegie in particular. This, it may be noted, was the interpretation generally placed upon the transaction in trade and financial circles at the time."

The price paid for the Carnegie Company, about April 1, 1901, was $492,006,160 in United States Steel Corporation securities — of the then market value of $447,416,640 in cash. The value of the actual assets of the Carnegie Company on December 31, 1899, as sworn to by Carnegie, had been only $75,610,104.06. The total assets of the concern on March 1, 1900, as shown by the balance sheet, were only $101,416,802.43. And Commissioner Herbert Knox Smith, making a very generous estimate of the net value of the tangible assets of the

Carnegie Company on April 1, 1901, fixes it at
only $197,563,000. The bribe paid to elimi-
nate Carnegie's efficiency was thus at least
$250,000,000. It was paid, as the Stanley Com-
mittee finds, to prevent a contest "between
fabricators of steel and fabricators of securities;
between makers of billets and of bonds." It
was paid to save the huge paper values which
George W. Perkins and others had recently created by combining into eight grossly overcapital-
ized corporations a large part of the steel mills of
America. No wonder that J. P. Morgan & Co.
were panic-stricken at the rumor that Carnegie
was to build a tube mill which might reduce the
cost of making tubes $10 a ton, when those
bankers had recently combined seventeen tube
mills (mostly old) of the aggregate value of
$19,000,000, had capitalized them at $80,000,000
and taken $20,000,000 of the securities for them-
selves as promotion fees. The seven other similar consolidations of steel plants floated about
the same time had an aggregate capitalization
of $437,825,800, of which $43,306,811 was
taken by the promoters for their fees.

As Commissioner Herbert Knox Smith reported to the President:

"A steel war might have meant the sudden end of
the extraordinary period of speculative activity and

profit. On the other hand, an averting of this war, and
the coalition of the various great consolidations, if
successfully financed, would be a tremendous 'bull'
argument. It would afford its promoters an opportunity for enormous stock-market profits through the
sale of securities."

So Carnegie was eliminated, and efficiency in
steel making was sacrificed in the interest of
Wall Street; the United States Steel Corporation was formed; and J. P. Morgan & Co.
and their associates took for their services as
promoters the additional sum of $62,500,000
in cash values.

THE SOURCES OF MOST PROFITS

The second proposition — that conspicuous
trust profits are due mainly to monopoly control
of the market — is supported by abundant evidence equally conclusive.

The Standard Oil Trust stood preëminent as
an excessive profit taker.

When Commissioner Herbert Knox Smith
made his report to President Roosevelt in 1907,
the trust had for a generation controlled about
eighty-seven per cent of the oil business of
America. It had throughout that period been
managed by men of unusual ability. And yet
Commissioner Smith reports:

"The conclusion is, therefore, irresistible that the real source of the Standard's power is not superior efficiency, but unfair and illegitimate practices. . . .

"Considering all the branches of the oil industry together, the difference in cost between the Standard and the independent concerns is not great. . . .

"It is true, that taken as a whole, the Standard Oil Company is a more efficient industrial machine than any one of its competitors. Nevertheless, careful estimates based upon data submitted by a number of independent concerns as to the cost of pipe-line transportation, refining, and distributing oil, as compared with the Standard's cost for these operations, indicate that the total difference in efficiency between the Standard and the independent concerns is not very great. . . .

"The difference between the operating cost of a number of Standard refineries and a number of independent refineries was shown to be substantially nothing. It is possible, however, that some of the larger Standard refineries are able to reduce their costs a little further and that there may be some difference in the amount required for profit per gallon. The Standard may also be able to secure somewhat better yields from the crude. It is improbable, however, as already stated, that the superior efficiency of the Standard with respect to both refining costs and yields would on the average represent a difference of more than one-fourth of a cent a gallon. The outside figure would be one-half cent per gallon.

"It has been shown further that the difference in marketing costs between Standard and independent concerns in large cities is almost negligible. . . .

"As already stated, moreover, the argument, from a comparison between the costs of the Standard and the costs of the present independent concerns, does not fully show the fallacy of the Standard's claim to have reduced prices by its superior efficiency. The present independent concerns are by no means so efficient as those which would have come into existence in the absence of the restraints imposed by the monopolistic and unfair methods of the Standard. Had the oil business continued to develop normally, it is practically certain that there would have been in the United States to-day a limited number of large oil concerns, the efficiency of which would be considerably greater than that of the present independents."

Next to the Standard Oil, the Tobacco Trust is, perhaps, the most prominent of the excessive profit takers. A single one of its many constituent companies, W. Duke's Sons & Co., "valued in 1885, under competition, at $250,-000," yielded to its owners "up to 1908, in securities, dividends, and interest" $39,000,000, or 156 times the value of this particular business in 1885. In 1908 (the latest year reported on by Commissioner Herbert Knox Smith) the profits of the Tobacco Trust equalled 39.5 per cent of its total tangible assets. But there are many different departments of the tobacco business; and the rate of profit was by no means the same in all in any one year. And in the same department the profits varied greatly during a series of years. In 1908, for instance, the profits of the cigar department were only 4 per cent on the value of the tangible assets, while the profits of the subsidiary smoking tobacco companies were 103.5 per cent of the value of the tangible assets. What is the explanation of this great variation in profits? The company was efficiently managed. The same able men supervised all of the departments. The same huge resources and trade influence were at the service of each of the departments. Commissioner Smith's elaborate investigation solves the riddle. It brings out clearly the following features:

"Very high rates of earnings on the actual investment in most departments.
"A marked coincidence of low rates of earnings and a low degree of control where the latter occurs.
"A remarkable increase in the rates of earnings as the combination became more effective in its control."

In 1908, when the trust earned only 4 per cent on its cigar business, it controlled only about one-eighth of the cigar business of the country. When it earned 103.5 per cent on its smoking tobacco subsidiaries, it controlled three-quarters of the smoking tobacco business of the country.

"The most striking feature of the entire preceding discussion," says Commissioner Smith in concluding, "is the almost invariable association of high rates of profit with a high degree of control, or with monopolistic conditions, and of lower rates of profit with a lesser degree of control or active competition. . . .

" The combination's ability to establish and maintain prices without much regard to competition in the principal branches of the business, it may be repeated, is vividly illustrated by the fact that when the internal-revenue tax on tobacco was reduced in 1901 and 1902, the combination maintained its prices at the level which had been established when the tax was increased some years earlier. As a result of this policy it appropriated practically the entire reduction in the tax as additional profit in succeeding years."

That is the kind of efficiency in which trusts particularly excel.

As to the Steel Trust's extraordinary profits, the Stanley Investigating Committee finds:

"The enormous earnings of the Steel Corporation are due not to a degree of integration or efficiency not possessed by its competitors, but to the ownership of ore reserves out of all proportion to its output or requirements, and to the control and operation

of common carriers, divisions of rates, and the liberal
allowance obtained from other concerns through inequitable and inordinate terminal allowances."

The third proposition — that trusts are not
efficient enough to hold their relative positions
in the trade as compared with the independents
without buying up successful competitors —
is also supported by abundant evidence.

The Steel Trust furnishes a striking example
of this. Corporation Commissioner Herbert
Knox Smith, reporting on the operations of the
Steel Trust for the ten years following its formation (1901–10), says:

"Notwithstanding the great additions made by
the corporation to its properties from earnings, and
the acquisition of several important competing concerns [including the Tennessee Coal and Iron Com-
pany], its proportion of the business in nearly every
important product, except pig iron and steel rails,
is less than it was in 1901. . . .

"This table shows that, whereas the Steel Corporation in 1910 had fully maintained the share of the
country's total production of pig iron it held in 1901,
its proportion of the production of nearly all steel products had declined, and in most cases sharply declined. The only important exception was steel rails.
The maintenance of its proportion here is chiefly

due to the erection of a very large rail mill at the new Gary plant, and to the acquisition of the Tennessee Coal, Iron and Railroad Company, which had a considerable steel-rail production.

"Taking the production of steel ingots and castings as a basis, it will be seen that the Steel Corporation's percentage of the total fell from 65.7 per cent in 1901 to 54.3 per cent in 1910. This figure, perhaps, is the best single criterion by which to judge the change in the corporation's position in the steel industry from a producing standpoint. . . . It should be noted that the decline in the production shown by this comparison of 1901 and 1910 percentages was practically continuous for most products throughout the entire period."

That was the condition in 1910. A year later the Steel Trust's proportion of the production of the country had fallen below fifty per cent.

It may be doubted whether steel rails would have been an "exception" to the steady decline in the Steel Corporation's proportion of the country's business had it not been for the steel-rail pool and the close community of interest between the Steel Corporation and the railroads. As the Stanley Committee finds:

"Of the $18,417,132,238 invested in railways in the United States, the directors of the Steel Corporation have a voice in the directorates of or act as executive officers of railroad companies with a total capitalization and bonded indebtedness of $10,365,771,833."

The Sugar Trust, also, furnishes striking evidence of the inability of trusts to maintain their position in the trade without buying up successful competitors. In 1892, after acquiring the Spreckels Company of the West, the Sugar Trust alone produced ninety per cent of the sugar refined in this country. It had vast resources. It had strong political affiliations. It sought by every means, fair or foul, to maintain its control. It secured discriminating rates from railroads. It cheated the Government by false weights and undervaluation. With the bankers' aid it crushed competitors through tricky control of credits. But in 1912 — at the end of twenty years of oppression — its own production of refined sugar had fallen to forty-two per cent of the country's production. And, in spite of buying up from time to time stock in so-called independent cane sugar companies and beet sugar companies, it controlled in 1912 (according to the statement of President Van Hise in "Concentration and Control") only sixty-two per cent of this country's production of refined sugar.

The dominating position of the Tobacco Trust

was likewise maintained only through its policy of buying up competitors, as Corporation Commissioner Herbert Knox Smith so clearly shows:

"Despite enormous expenditures for advertising and in 'schemes,' and despite frequent price cutting by means of its so-called 'fighting brands' and its bogus independent concerns, there has been in several branches of the industry a constant tendency for competitors to gain business more rapidly than the combination, and thus to reduce its proportion of the output. This tendency has been overcome only by continued buying up of competitive concerns. Many weaker concerns have been virtually driven out of business or forced to sell out to the combination, either by reason of the direct competition of the latter, or as an indirect result of the vigorous competition between the combination and larger independent concerns. In the case of the larger and more powerful concerns which it acquired, however, the combination has usually secured control only by paying a high price. The immense profits of the combination have enabled it to keep up this policy.

"This great disparity in size [between the factories of the combination and those of the independents] is not due to lack of enterprise or capital on the part of the independent concerns, but is essentially due to the constant transfer of the largest concerns from the ranks of the independents to those of the combination. . . .

"The output of individual concerns that remained

independent, however, has increased in most instances. The resultant tendency to increase the entire independent output was offset by the combination's continued policy of buying up and absorbing the larger and more successful competitors."

Even the Standard Oil Trust, which relied mainly upon its control of the transportation systems and other methods of unfair competition to crush competitors, is shown by Commissioner Smith to have been unable to quite maintain its relative position in the market, despite its continued buying up of competitors.

UNSUCCESSFUL TRUSTS

Of the truth of the fourth proposition, stated above — that most of the trusts which did not secure monopolistic positions have failed to show marked success or efficiency as compared with the independent competing concerns — every reader familiar with business must be able to supply evidence. Let him who doubts examine the stock quotations of long-established industrials and look particularly at the common stock which ordinarily represents the "expected economies" or "efficiency" of combination. Take as examples:

The Upper Leather Trust (American Hide and Leather Company — a combination of twenty-one different concerns), with common at 5¼ and preferred at 26¾.

The Sole Leather Trust (Central Leather Company — a combination of over sixty tanneries), with common at 26.

The Paper Trust (International Paper Company — a combination of twenty-three news mills), with common at 10.

The Paper Bag Trust (Union Bag and Paper Company — a combination of seven different concerns), with common at 6⅝.

The Writing Paper Trust (American Writing Paper Company — a combination of twenty-eight different concerns), with preferred at 28½ and common at 3¾ — almost below the horizon of a quotation.

But perhaps the most conspicuous industrial trust which was not able to secure control of the market is the International Mercantile Marine. That company had behind it the ability and resources of J. P. Morgan & Co., and their great influence with the railroads. It secured a working agreement with the Hamburg American, the North German Lloyd and other companies; but it could not secure control of the Atlantic trade, and in the seven years since its organization has not paid a dividend on its $100,000,000 of stock. Its common stands at 5⅛, its preferred at 18⅞, and they stood little better before the *Titanic* disaster. On the other hand, the $120,000,000 stock of the Pullman Company, which has like influence with the railroads but succeeded in securing a monopoly, stands at 170¾.

Efficient or inefficient, every company which controls the market is a "money-maker." No, the issue of "Competition *versus* Monopoly" cannot be distorted into the issue of "Small Concerns *versus* Large." The unit in business may, of course, be too small to be efficient, and the larger unit has been a common incident of monopoly. But a unit too small for efficiency is by no means a necessary incident of competition. And a unit *too large* to be efficient is no uncommon incident of monopoly. Man's work often outruns the capacity of the individual man; and no matter how good the organization, the capacity of an individual man usually determines the success or failure of a particular enterprise — not only financially to the owners but in service to the community. Organization can do much to make concerns more efficient. Organization can do much to make larger units possible and profitable. But the efficacy even of organization has its bounds. There is a point where the centrifugal force necessarily exceeds the centripetal. And organization can never supply the combined judgment, initiative, enterprise and authority which must come from the chief executive officer.   Nature sets a limit to his possible achievement.

As the Germans say: "Care is taken that the trees do not scrape the skies."

TRUSTS AND THE EXPORT TRADE[1]

PROGRESSIVE PARTY advocates of legalizing industrial monopolies urge as a reason the necessities of the export trade. "How can we," say they, "compete with small concerns against England and Germany for the commerce of the world?"

The answer is not difficult. There is no such alternative as "monopoly or the small concern." America has to-day, in all lines of competitive business, concerns large enough to be the most efficient instruments of commerce, be it foreign or domestic. With America's abundant capital and the ambition of its citizens, there will be no lack of "bigness" in industry. We need not legalize monopoly in order to equip ourselves for the foreign trade.

A survey of the relations of our leading trusts to the export trade should dispel the belief that we are particularly indebted to them either for the quantity or character of their foreign business.

[1] Published in "Collier's Weekly," September 21, 1912.

STEEL

First. Take the exports of steel — the crude products in which the Steel Trust deals. George W. Perkins, so prominent as promoter and director of that corporation, gravely told the Senate Committee: "We have been infinitely more successful in expanding our foreign trade than would have been possible under competitive conditions." But the facts show that the organization of the Steel Trust arrested the development of the American export trade in steel. Our cost of production rose, while that of European steel makers remained stationary and they gained the world's growing trade.

The Steel Trust was organized April 1, 1901. During the ten years, 1901 to 1910, our exports of crude steel and iron products increased from 1,154,000 to 1,533,000 tons, or 33 per cent; Great Britain's from 3,213,000 to 4,594,000, or 43 per cent; Germany's from 838,000 to 4,868,-000, or 480 per cent. In other words, America had in 1901, as compared with England and Germany, nearly 22 per cent of the world's export tonnage. In 1910 America had less than 13 per cent. During these ten years coincident with the existence of the Steel Trust, America lost steadily in prestige in the world's steel market.

As stated by Mr. T. Good in his able discussion of the subject:

"From the moment that the Steel Trust got to work the American iron and steel industry was diverted from natural to unnatural developments. Costs and prices of raw material were inflated; progress toward economy was arrested; retrogression set in and America's rosy chances of annexing the world's export trade were shattered. . . . It is, indeed, a demonstrable fact that the trust has done more harm than good from an American point of view; that it has burdened and handicapped the American steel trade, and incidentally given Britain, Germany and other countries better chances in the race. Last year, 1910, the British iron and steel exports were further in advance of those of America than they were in 1900, the year before the Steel Trust got down to business; while German exports, which were about thirty per cent below those of the United States in 1900, are now something like three hundred per cent above them."

And the Steel Trust's foreign sales were no more satisfactory in character than in quantity. Export prices were almost uniformly lower than domestic prices, and in some instances the advantage given foreign consumers was surprisingly large, the five-year average being, as the

Stanley Committee shows, for steel rails about $4 a ton, for structural shapes over $5 a ton, and for tin plates over $14.50 a ton.

Steel Trust officials endeavor to meet this damaging evidence and to support their assertion that the trust has benefited our export trade by presenting the following facts: (1) The trust exports more steel than its constituent companies did before the trust was organized. (2) The trust's percentage of the total crude steel exports of the country, as compared with the independents, has risen greatly and now amounts to ninety-five per cent of the total exports of that character. (3) The trust's exports increased largely in 1911 over 1910.

The facts adduced by the trust's officials, rightly interpreted, tend rather to disprove than to prove their contention. The reason why America lost its prestige in the world's steel trade was the huge increase in the cost of producing steel in America. That increased cost was due particularly to the increased cost of producing pig iron. And for the increased cost of pig iron the organization of the Steel Trust is in large part responsible. That increase cost drove the independents out of the foreign market where prices are competitive; and they necessarily confined themselves to the domestic

market where prices were maintained through
Gary dinners.   The Steel Trust could still sell
abroad, because its ownership of transportation systems gave them an unfair advantage
over the independents. The trust was perhaps
driven to sell some of its product abroad, because the independents made such heavy inroads upon the trust's percentage of the domestic business — reducing it from over sixty per
cent in 1901 to less than fifty per cent in 1911.

The large increase of exports of the trust in
1911 was due, in part, to the sharp fall in the
selling price of steel in the United States during
that year.   And the price fell, doubtless, not
so much because of lessened demand as because the Stanley Committee investigation led
to the discontinuance of the Gary dinners.

America may well take pride in her large exports of iron and steel products. In 1910 they
amounted to $201,271,903; in 1911 to $249,-
656,411.   But it is the highly manufactured
iron and steel products, made largely under
competitive conditions, like tools and machinery,
to which these large totals are mainly due.
The Steel Trust's exports in 1910 amounted
(as the Stanley Committee finds) to only $41,-
586,950.   Machinery and machines rose from
$50,897,390 in 1902 to $111,135,833 in 1911.

The growth of exports in highly manufactured iron and steel products is the more remarkable in view of the handicap to which our manufactures are subjected through the Steel Trust by the high prices for crude steel products.

Furthermore, the Steel Trust claims to supply ninety-five per cent of our crude steel exports. If the formation of trusts advances the export trade, why have we fallen behind Germany and England in steel exports? Surely they have no steel trusts comparable with the Steel Corporation in size or resources.

Progressive Party advocates of monopoly have the habit of attributing the commercial development of Germany largely to the size of their industrial units and to the legalization of monopolies; but they misread the facts.

One of the largest and most successful of the German cartels is that of the steel producers, controlling ninety-five per cent of the country's production — as our Steel Trust controls ninety-five per cent of this country's crude steel exports. The German Trust consists of thirty-six separate concerns. Their aggregate capital is a little over 1,250,000,000 marks, or $312,000,000 — much less than one-fourth of the capitalization of the United States Steel Corporation, which, including underlying bonds and outstanding securities of subsidiary companies, is found by the Stanley Committee to be $1,465,555,819. The average capital of each of those thirty-six German concerns is less than $10,000,000; and probably not one of them has a capital as large as some of our so-called independents; for the Lackawanna Steel Company has a capitalization in bonds and stocks of $145,412,000; the Republic Iron & Steel Co., $70,630,000; the Cambria Steel Company, $59,468,000; the Jones & Laughlin Steel Company, $54,487,000; and the Bethlehem Steel Company, $66,336,000.

Furthermore, each one of those thirty-six German concerns, which are federated for certain purposes, are free and independent in other respects. They are restricted as to selling price and quantity of production (these being fixed by the syndicate), but they are absolutely independent as to internal management. The syndicate exercises no control whatever as to methods and processes of manufacture, or over the method of securing raw material by the individual members, or with their labor policy. Furthermore, the limited quota assigned to each member relates exclusively to products made for sale. Any member may use as much steel and iron as he pleases in his own factories; that is, may work up into more highly manufactured goods the crude steel products to which alone the cartel restrictions apply. The German Steel Trust preserved competition in large part among its constituent concerns. The United States Steel Trust destroyed competition among its constituent concerns. This greater freedom for individual action, coupled with the fact that the thirty-six concerns are separately owned, and that the combination agreement is for a limited term only, may account, in large part, for the fact that, in Germany, the cost of producing iron and steel is no higher than it was ten or twelve years ago, while the American cost of production has risen greatly.

How groundless, in the light of these facts, is the contention made by Mr. George W. Perkins, before the Senate Committee on Interstate Commerce, that the Steel Trust must be preserved to put us on a par with Germany:

"Suppose," asked Senator Newlands, "the steel company were divided to-day into ten corporations of $150,000,000 each, instead of being organized into one corporation having nearly a billion and a half of capital. Do you not think that each one of those units could be as efficient in business and in all the economies as the total aggregation in one corporation?"

"Not as efficient," answered Mr. Perkins. "If I were asked to put my finger on one disadvantage greater than the other, it would be its effect on the foreign trade. You take ten such companies and go out and compete with Germany. It is self-evident that we could not begin to do it as effectively as with one large company."

But the ultimate success even of the German competitive system of combinations is by no means assured. Although a very wide field of competitive endeavor is left open and the incentive of separate ownership is preserved, the evils of combination appear not to have been entirely avoided. The steel and iron cartel was not formed until 1904; but already (as the statement quoted by President Van Hise in his "Concentration and Control" shows) grave difficulties are manifesting themselves:

"It is feared that the organization of the steel industry in the form of the steel combine will result in a gradual deterioration in the quality of steel products and that the chief object of the combine will become quantity rather than quality.

"It is maintained that the wishes of customers are not given due consideration; that they are compelled to take the quality of steel which the combine sees fit to give them, regardless of the special needs of their business; . . . that it is difficult for the manufacturer to secure as uniform a grade of goods as he had been able to obtain when he bought all his steel from the same firm. . . .

"The combine has . . . secured gradually increasing prices. . . .

"It is also asserted that . . . it has been possible for the cartel to shift the burden more and more upon the less organized manufacturers who use steel products as raw materials. Consequently the last and unorganized stages of steel products manufacture — *e. g.*, machine-making, etc. — have been forced to bear the greater proportion of the burden caused by a gradual increase in prices. These manufacturers will undoubtedly be able to shift a part of the burden upon the final consumer. . . ."

It is notable that the combination sells steel abroad lower than at home; in some cases as much as twenty per cent cheaper, following the same policy as the United States Steel Corporation.

"The manufacturing interests claim, and apparently with good grounds, that the export policy of the steel combine will in the long run prove disastrous to the exports of the German machine industries. Whenever the home market is unable to absorb the amount of steel that the producers place at the syndicate's disposal, it is generally forced to reduce its price to foreign buyers in order to get rid of the output. In this way the foreign manufacturer of machines, by obtaining his raw material from the German combine, is placed in an unduly advantageous position in competing with the German producer. In 1904, for example, pig iron was sold abroad at from 69 to 70 marks, whereas the domestic buyer was forced to pay from 82½ to 92½. . . .

"Generally the larger and more powerful members have benefited more than the weaker ones, through its activity; and in some cases the condition of the weaker members has deteriorated rather than improved. While some companies have undoubtedly been able to remain in existence as a result of the syndicate's activity that would under the competitive system have been forced to the wall, others that might have developed under the competitive system have been held back by the cartel's policy of combination."

Has n't all that a very familiar sound? "Gradually increasing prices"; "shifting the burden upon the ultimate consumer"; "selling cheaper abroad than at home." Verily, if the tariff is not the "Mother of the Trusts," the attendant abuses are at least akin.

OIL

Second. Take next the export of mineral oil and oil products — a very important item in our exports. In 1911 it amounted in value to $105,922,848, or about one-twentieth of our total exports. The exports are, also, a very important part of America's oil trade, as we have customarily exported more than one-half of all the illuminating oil produced in the country. For more than a generation the Standard Oil

Company dominated the American oil trade, having in recent years about eighty-six per cent of the business of the country. That company stood preëminent among American trusts in age, in power, in resources, in perfection of organization, and in ability of management. Through the unfair use of that power, ability and organization it prevented the rise of any large American competitor. If great size and monopoly powers gave peculiar advantages to Americans for developing export trade, surely the Standard should have conquered for us the oil trade of the world; but Corporation Commissioner Herbert Knox Smith showed that, though our oil exports grew largely, we lost during the reign of the Standard Oil our relative position in the world's market, adding:

"More than half the illuminating oil produced in this country is exported. The exportation of naphtha, lubricating oils, paraffin, wax and candles made from wax is also considerable. This country is, however, to-day a comparatively less important factor in the petroleum markets of the world than it was twenty or thirty years ago."

And Commissioner Herbert Knox Smith also shows that the Standard Oil Company did not succeed in acquiring any larger part of the foreign trade than it did of the domestic, the percentage in each being about eighty-seven per cent of the whole, saying:

"The percentage of export trade in illuminating oil handled or controlled by the Standard Oil Company, therefore, is substantially the same as the proportion of its production."

And, like the Steel Trust, the Standard Oil was persistently selling its product much cheaper abroad than in America, imposing extra burdens upon the American consumer to compensate for any possible losses in the foreign trade, as Commissioner Herbert Knox Smith so clearly shows:

"The preceding analysis of the price policy of the Standard Oil Company in the export trade during recent years, as compared with its price policy in the domestic trade, shows two conspicuous facts. In the first place, while the prices of illuminating oil in the principal foreign markets have for years been relatively lower than the prices in the United States, this disparity became especially conspicuous during the years 1903, 1904 and 1905. During those years the domestic prices stood at a much higher level than for many years before, while prices in the principal foreign markets, like the United Kingdom, Germany and the Orient, stood at times from two to three cents below the average price in the United States, transportation costs, difference in quality of oil, etc., being taken into account.

"In the second place, the investigation shows that the decrease in prices in the foreign trade, during the years 1903–1905, was not due to an oversupply of American oil or the oil from all sources combined, but was due particularly to an attack by the Standard Oil Company upon certain new and threatening competitors. Aside from other proofs, conclusive evidence that there was no oversupply of American oil, as well as evidence that the Standard's policy has been to promote its own interests rather than those of the United States, is found in the Standard's extensive purchases of Russian oil during these years and its acquisition of crude-oil land and refineries in foreign countries."

President Van Hise, in his "Concentration and Control," mentions that in 1905 the United States was taken into the International Steel Rail Syndicate, and also says:

"Oil is one of the businesses in which the international combination and co-operation have gone far, in some cases there being union, in others division, of territory."

Possibly these facts may furnish a partial explanation of America's falling prestige in the foreign steel and oil trades. Was the foreign market sacrificed to avoid competition by the foreigners in the domestic market?

TOBACCO

Third. Tobacco presents a field where an important foreign market was deliberately sacrificed by the dominating trust in order to protect itself from foreign competition in the home market. Tobacco products are among our leading manufactures, but our exports of manufactured tobacco products are, as Commissioner Herbert Knox Smith reports, "comparatively insignificant."

"The exports in 1908 amounted to $5,550,695, or less than two per cent of the value of our manufactures of tobacco. . . . [In 1911 they amounted to only $4,677,859.]

"The existence of governmental monopolies of tobacco manufactures in a number of leading countries and of prohibitive tariffs on the importation of manufactured tobacco in other countries prevents any considerable development in international trade in such products."

The Tobacco Trust, which acquired control of the greater part of what little of the export trade America had, deliberately closed the door to any exports by it to Great Britain or Ireland. In consideration of the powerful British trust (the Imperial) agreeing not to carry on business in manufactured tobaccos in

the United States, the Tobacco Trust, and its
active directors individually, agreed that they
would not thereafter, directly or indirectly,
carry on business in Great Britain or Ireland.

WHY EXPORTS GROW

Trusts have, of course, contributed to our export trade, as have many independent manufacturers. Some of these trust contributions
have been large; but the great increase in our
exports of manufactures is not due to the existence of trusts. Increased exports have been
quite as marked in other lines as in trust-made
goods. We hear particularly of the Harvester
Trust's export business; and it is true that this
country's exports in agricultural implements
doubled in ten years — 1902 to 1911. But in
many long-established and highly competitive
lines of manufacture, like special lines of machinery and of tools, the 1911 exports were not
only double but threefold those of 1902; and in
other new and highly competitive businesses the
increases were much greater. For instance, the
1911 exports of automobiles were twenty times
as large as those of 1902; the 1912 exports
nearly thirty times as large. The fact is we
have become a great manufacturing people. In
the year ending June 30, 1912, our exports of

manufactured products exceeded $1,000,000,000.
American manufactures have been developed
through initiative, enterprise, energy and ambition — all common characteristics of competitive business. The trusts had, of course, a
part in securing these foreign markets; and
have enjoyed, perhaps, a still larger share of
their fruits by exploiting foreign markets in
which independent manufacturers had been the
pioneers.

But the trusts have not been the cause of our
heavy export business; nor are they essential to
its continuance or future development. And
it should be borne in mind that the great
trusts carry, in their huge resources and the
volume of their business, also an element of danger to our export trade. Many of them have
already established factories in foreign countries from which they supply a part, at least, of
their foreign trade. This is true of the Standard Oil Company, of the Harvester Company,
of the Shoe Machinery Company and of many
others. The establishment of these foreign factories has been due, in large measure, to the
existence of foreign tariffs or to the requirements of foreign patent laws. But it has been
due, in part, also to a lower cost of production
abroad, resulting from the lower wages paid

there. We have been able, in many lines, to produce goods at lower cost in America than foreigners do abroad, in spite of paying higher wages; because of greater superiority in management or the introduction of advanced machinery and labor-saving devices. But is it not possible that our able business managers, transferring to foreign countries American business organization, machinery and methods, may be able to produce with low-priced foreign labor goods for the foreign trade more cheaply abroad than at home? And, in such event, would they not be led to develop their foreign factories instead of those at home, and the export trade suffer accordingly? Such a course might bring great gains to the American capitalists, who are the stockholders of the trusts; but the American workingmen would lose.

Has not our export trade more to lose than to gain through the legalization of monopolies?

COMPETITION THAT KILLS[1]

"I CANNOT believe," said Mr. Justice Holmes, "that in the long run the public will profit by this course, permitting knaves to cut reasonable prices for mere ulterior purposes of their own, and thus to impair, if not destroy, the production and the sale of articles which it is assumed to be desirable the people should be able to get."

Such was the dissent registered by this forward-looking judge when, two years ago, the Supreme Court of the United States declared invalid contracts by which a manufacturer of trade-marked goods sought to prevent retailers from cutting the price he had established.[2] Shortly before, the court had held that mere possession of a copyright did not give the maker of an article power to fix by notice the price at which it should be sold to the consumer.[3] And now the court, by a five-to-four decision, has applied the same rule to patented articles, thus dealing a third blow at the practice of

---

[1] Published in "Harper's Weekly," November 15, 1913.
[2] Dr. Miles Medical Co. *vs.* Park & Sons Co., 220 U. S. 409.
[3] Bobbs-Merrill Co. *vs.* Straus, 210 U. S. 339.

retailing nationally advertised goods at a uniform price throughout the country.[1]

Primitive barter was a contest of wits instead of an exchange of ascertained values. It was, indeed, an equation of two unknown quantities. Trading took its first great advance when money was adopted as the medium of exchange. That removed one-half of the uncertainty incident to a trade; but only one-half. The transaction of buying and selling remained still a contest of wits. The seller still gave as little in value and got as much in money as he could. And the law looked on at the contest, declaring solemnly and ominously: "Let the buyer beware." Within ample limits the seller might legally lie with impunity; and, almost without limits, he might legally deceive by silence. The law gave no redress because it deemed reliance upon sellers' talk unreasonable; and not to discover for one's self the defects in an article purchased was ordinarily proof of negligence. A good bargain meant a transaction in which one person got the better of another. Trading in the "good old days" imposed upon the seller no obligation either to tell the truth, or to give value or to treat all customers alike. But in the last generation trade morals have made

[1] Bauer *vs.* O'Donnell, 229 U. S. 1.

great strides. New methods essential to doing business on a large scale were introduced. They are time-saving and labor-saving; and have proved also conscience-saving devices.

The greatest progress in this respect has been made in the retail trade; and the first important step was the introduction of the one-price store. That eliminated the constant haggling about prices, and the unjust discrimination among customers. But it did far more. It tended to secure fair prices; for it compelled the dealer to make, deliberately, prices by which he was prepared to stand or fall. It involved a publicity of prices which invited a comparison in detail with those of competitors; and it subjected all his prices to the criticism of all his customers. But while the one-price store marked a great advance, it did not bring the full assurance that the seller was giving value. The day's price of the article offered was fixed and every customer was treated alike; but there was still no adequate guarantee of value, both because there was ordinarily no recognized standard of quality for the particular article, and because there was no standard price even for the article of standard quality.

Under such conditions the purchaser had still to rely for protection on his own acumen, or on the character and judgment of the retailer; and the individual producer had little encouragement to establish or to maintain a reputation. The unscrupulous or unskilful dealer might be led to abandon his goods for cheaper and inferior substitutes. This ever-present danger led to an ever-widening use of trade-marks. Thereby the producer secured the reward for well-doing and the consumer the desired guarantee of quality. Later the sale of trade-marked goods at retail in original packages supplied a further assurance of quality, and also the assurance that the proper quantity was delivered. The enactment of the Federal Pure Food law and similar State legislation strengthened these guarantees.

But the standard of value in retail trade was not fully secured until a method was devised by which a uniform retail selling price was established for trade-marked articles sold in the original package. In that way, widely extended use of a trade-marked article fostered by national advertising could create both a reputation for the article and a common knowledge of its established selling price or value. With the introduction of that device the evolution of the modern purchase became complete. The ordinary retail sale — the transaction which had

once been an equation of two unknown quantities — became an equation of two known
quantities. Uncertainty in trade is eliminated
by "A Dollar and the Ingersoll Watch," or
"Five cents and the Uneeda Biscuits."

THE COURT'S PROHIBITION

Such is the one-price system to which the
United States Supreme Court denied its sanc-
tion. The courts of Great Britain had recognized this method of marketing goods as legal.
The Supreme Court of Massachusetts and that
of California had approved it. The system was
introduced into America many years ago, and
has become widely extended. To abandon it now
would disturb many lines of business and seriously impair the prosperity of many concerns.

When the United States Supreme Court denied to makers of copyrighted or patented goods
the power to fix by notice the prices at which the
goods should be retailed, the court merely interpreted the patent and copyright acts and declared that they do not confer any such special
privilege. But when the court denied the validity of contracts for price-maintenance of trade-
marked goods, it decided a very different matter.
It did not rest its decision mainly upon the
interpretation of a statute; for there is no stat-

ute which in terms prohibits price-maintenance, or, indeed, deals directly with the subject. It did not refuse to grant a special privilege to certain manufacturers; it denied a common right to all producers. Nor does the decision of the court proceed upon any fundamental or technical rule of law. The decision rests mainly upon general reasoning as to public policy; and that reasoning is largely from analogy.

THE DEMANDS OF PUBLIC POLICY

When a court decides a case upon grounds of public policy, the judges become, in effect, legislators. The question then involved is no longer one for lawyers only. It seems fitting, therefore, to inquire whether this judicial legislation is sound — whether the common trade practice of maintaining the price of trade-marked articles has been justly condemned. And when making that inquiry we may well bear in mind this admonition of Sir George Jessel, a very wise English judge:

"If there is one thing which more than any other public policy requires, it is that men of full age and competent understanding shall have the utmost liberty of contracting, and that their contracts, when entered into freely and voluntarily, shall be held sacred, and shall be enforced by courts of justice.

Therefore, you have this paramount public policy to consider, that you are not lightly to interfere with this freedom of contract."

THE COURT'S OBJECTION

The Supreme Court says that a contract by which a producer binds a retailer to maintain the established selling price of his trade-marked product is void; because it prevents competition between retailers of the article and restrains trade.

Such a contract does, in a way, limit competition; but no man is bound to compete with himself. And when the same trade-marked article is sold in the same market by one dealer at a less price than by another, the producer, in effect, competes with himself. To avoid such competition, the producer of a trade-marked article often sells it to but a single dealer in a city or town; or he establishes an exclusive sales agency. No one has questioned the legal right of an independent producer to create such exclusive outlets for his product. But if exclusive selling agencies are legal, why should the individual manufacturer of a trade-marked article be prevented from establishing a marketing system under which his several agencies for distribution will sell at the same price?

There is no difference, in substance, between an agent who retails the article and a dealer who retails it.

For many business concerns the policy of maintaining a standard price for a standard article is simple. The village baker readily maintained the quality and price of his product, by sale and delivery over his own counter. The great Standard Oil monopoly maintains quality and price (when it desires so to do) by selling throughout the world to the retailer or the consumer from its own tank-wagons. But for most producers the jobber and the retailer are the necessary means of distribution—as necessary as the railroad, the express or the parcel post. The Standard Oil Company can, without entering into contracts with dealers, maintain the price through its dominant power. Shall the law discriminate against the lesser concerns which have not that power, and deny them the legal right to contract with dealers to accomplish a like result? For in order to insure to the small producer the ability to maintain the price of his product, the law must afford him contract protection, when he deals through the middleman.

But the Supreme Court says that a contract which prevents a dealer of trade-marked articles from cutting the established selling price, restrains trade. In a sense every contract restrains trade; for after one has entered into a contract, he is not as free in trading as he was before he bound himself. But the right to bind one's self is essential to trade development. And it is not every contract in restraint of trade, but only contracts *unreasonably* in restraint of trade, which are invalid. Whether a contract does unreasonably restrain trade is not to be determined by abstract reasoning. Facts only can be safely relied upon to teach us whether a trade practice is consistent with the general welfare. And abundant experience establishes that the one-price system, which marks so important an advance in the ethics of trade, has also greatly increased the efficiency of merchandising, not only for the producer, but for the dealer and the consumer as well.

THE PRODUCER'S PLEA

If a dealer is selling unknown goods or goods under his own name, he alone should set the price; but when a dealer has to use somebody else's name or brand in order to sell goods, then the owner of that name or brand has an interest which should be respected. The transaction is essentially one between the two principals —

the maker and the user. All others are middlemen or agents; for the product is not really
sold until it has been bought by the consumer.
Why should one middleman have the power to
depreciate in the public mind the value of the
maker's brand and render it unprofitable not
only for the maker but for other middlemen?
Why should one middleman be allowed to in-
dulge in a practice of price-cutting, which tends
to drive the maker's goods out of the market
and in the end interferes with people getting
the goods at all?

CUT PRICES A MISLEADER

When a trade-marked article is advertised to
be sold at less than the standard price, it is generally done to attract persons to the particular
store by the offer of an obviously extraordinary
bargain. It is a bait — called by the dealers
a "leader." But the cut-price article would
more appropriately be termed a "mis-leader";
because ordinarily the very purpose of the cut-
price is to create a false impression.

The dealer who sells the Dollar Ingersoll
watch for sixty-seven cents necessarily loses
money in that particular transaction. He has
no desire to sell any article on which he must
lose money. He advertises the sale partly to

attract customers to his store; but mainly to create in the minds of those customers the false impression that other articles in which he deals and which are not of a standard or known value will be sold upon like favorable terms.   The customer is expected to believe that if an Ingersoll watch is sold at thirty-three and one-third per cent less than others charge for it, a ready-to-wear suit or a gold ring will be sold as cheap. The more successful the individual producer of a trade-marked article has been in creating for it a recognized value as well as a wide sale, the greater is the temptation to the unscrupulous to cut the price.   Indeed a cut-price article can ordinarily be effective as a "mis-leader" only when both the merits and the established selling price are widely known.

HOW CUT PRICES HURT

The evil results of price-cutting are far-reaching.   It is sometimes urged that price-cutting of a trade-marked article injures no one; that the producer is not injured, since he received his full price in the original sale to jobber or retailer; and indeed may be benefited by increased sales, since lower prices ordinarily stimulate trade; that the retailer cannot be harmed, since he has cut the price voluntarily to advance his own interests; that the consumer is surely benefited because he gets the article cheaper. But this reasoning is most superficial and misleading.

To sell a Dollar Ingersoll watch for sixty-seven cents injures both the manufacturer and the regular dealer; because it tends to make the public believe that either the manufacturer's or the dealer's profits are ordinarily exorbitant; or, in other words, that the watch is not worth a dollar. Such a cut necessarily impairs the reputation of the article, and, by impairing reputation, lessens the demand. It may even destroy the manufacturer's market. A few conspicuous "cut-price sales" in any market will demoralize the trade of the regular dealers in that article. They cannot sell it at cut prices without losing money. They might be able to sell a few of the articles at the established price; but they would do so at the risk to their own reputations. The cut by others, if known, would create the impression on their own customers of having been overcharged. It is better policy for the regular dealer to drop the line altogether. On the other hand, the demand for the article from the irregular dealer who cuts the price is short-lived. The cut-price article cannot long remain his "leader."

His use for it is sporadic and temporary. One "leader" is soon discarded for another. Then the cut-price outlet is closed to the producer; and, meanwhile, the regular trade has been lost. Thus a single prominent price-cutter can ruin a market for both the producer and the regular retailer. And the loss to the retailer is serious.

On the other hand, the consumer's gain from price-cutting is only sporadic and temporary. The few who buy a standard article for less than its value do benefit — unless they have, at the same time, been misled into buying some other article at more than its value. But the public generally is the loser; and the losses are often permanent. If the price-cutting is not stayed, and the manufacturer reduces the price to his regular customers in order to enable them to retain their market, he is tempted to deteriorate the article in order to preserve his own profits. If the manufacturer cannot or will not reduce his price to the dealer, and the regular retailers abandon the line, the consumer suffers at least the inconvenience of not being able to buy the article.

PRICE MAINTENANCE — NOT PRICE FIXING

The independent producer of an article which bears his name or trade-mark — be he manufacturer or grower — seeks no special privilege when he makes contracts to prevent retailers from cutting his established selling price. The producer says in effect: "That which I create, in which I embody my experience, to which I give my reputation, is my property. By my own effort I have created a product valuable not only to myself, but to the consumer; for I have endowed this specific article with qualities which the consumer desires, and which the consumer should be able to rely confidently upon receiving when he purchases my article in the original package. To be able to buy my article with the assurance that it possesses the desired qualities is quite as much of value to the consumer who purchases it as it is of value to the maker who is seeking to find customers for it. It is essential that the consumer should have confidence, not only in the quality of my product, but in the fairness of the price he pays. And to accomplish a proper and adequate distribution of product, guaranteed both as to quality and price, I must provide by contract against the retail price being cut."

The position of the independent producer who establishes the price at which his own trademarked article shall be sold to the consumer must not be confused with that of a combination or trust which, controlling the market, fixes the price of a staple article. The independent producer is engaged in a business open to competition. He establishes his price at his peril — the peril that, if he sets it too high, either the consumer will not buy, or, if the article is nevertheless popular, the high profits will invite even more competition. The consumer who pays the price established by an independent producer in a competitive line of business does so voluntarily; he pays the price asked, because he deems the article worth that price as compared with the cost of other competing articles. But when a trust fixes, through its monopoly power, the price of a staple article in common use, the consumer does not pay the price voluntarily. He pays under compulsion. There being no competitor he must pay the price fixed by the trust, or be deprived of the use of the article.

PRICE–CUTTING THE ROAD TO MONOPOLY

Price-cutting has, naturally, played a prominent part in the history of nearly every American industrial monopoly.

Commissioner Herbert Knox Smith found, after the elaborate investigation undertaken by the Federal Bureau of Corporations, that:

"One of the most effective means employed by the Standard Oil Company to secure and maintain the large degree of monopoly which it possesses, is the cut in prices to the particular customers, or in the particular markets of its competitors, while maintaining them at a higher level elsewhere."

And Chief Justice White, in delivering the opinion of the United States Supreme Court in the Tobacco Trust case, said:

". . . the intention existed to use the power of the combination as a vantage ground to further monopolize the trade in tobacco by means of trade conflicts designed to injure others, either by driving competitors out of the business or compelling them to become parties to a combination — a purpose whose execution was illustrated by the plug war which ensued and its results, by the snuff war which followed and its results, and by the conflict which immediately followed the entry of the combination in England and the division of the world's business by the two foreign contracts which ensued."

Therefore recent legislative attempts to stay monopoly commonly include in some form prohibition against the making of cut-throat prices, with a view to suppressing competition. Such provisions will be found in the bills proposed by Senator La Follette, Congressman Stanley and Senator Cummins to supplement the Sherman

Anti-Trust Act; and statutes dealing with the subject have been enacted in several States.

President Wilson urged most wisely that, instead of sanctioning and regulating private monopoly, we should regulate competition. Undoubtedly statutes must be enacted to secure adequate and effective regulation; but shall our courts prohibit voluntary regulation of competition by those engaged in business? And is not the one-price system for trade-marked articles a most desirable form of regulation?

MONOPOLY'S EASIEST WAY

The competition attained by prohibiting the producer of a trade-marked article from maintaining his established price offers nothing substantial. Such competition is superficial merely. It is sporadic, temporary, delusive. It fails to protect the public where protection is needed. It is powerless to prevent the trust from fixing extortionate prices for its product. The great corporation with ample capital, a perfected organization and a large volume of business can establish its own agencies or sell direct to the consumer, and is in no danger of having its business destroyed by price-cutting among retailers. But the prohibition of price-maintenance imposes upon the small and independent

producers a serious handicap. Some avenue of
escape must be sought by them; and it may be
found in combination. Independent manufacturers without the capital or the volume of
business requisite for engaging alone in the
retail trade will be apt to combine with existing chains of stores, or to join with other manufacturers similarly situated in establishing new
chains of retail stores through which to market
their products direct to the consumer. The
process of exterminating the small independent
retailer already hard pressed by capitalistic
combinations — the mail-order houses, existing
chains of stores and the large department
stores — would be greatly accelerated by such
a movement. Already the displacement of the
small independent business man by the huge
corporation with its myriad of employees, its
absentee ownership and its financier control
presents a grave danger to our democracy. The
social loss is great; and there is no economic
gain. But the process of capitalizing free
Americans is not an inevitable one. It is not
even in accord with the natural law of business.
It is largely the result of unwise, man-made,
privilege-creating law, which has stimulated
existing tendencies to inequality instead of dis-
couraging them. Shall we, under the guise of

protecting competition, further foster monopoly by creating immunity for the price-cutters?

Americans should be under no illusions as to the value or effect of price-cutting. It has been the most potent weapon of monopoly — a means of killing the small rival to which the great trusts have resorted most frequently. It is so simple, so effective. Far-seeing organized capital secures by this means the co-operation of the short-sighted unorganized consumer to his own undoing. Thoughtless or weak, he yields to the temptation of trifling immediate gain, and, selling his birthright for a mess of pottage, becomes himself an instrument of monopoly.

THE NEW ENGLAND TRANSPORTA-
TION MONOPOLY

Mr. President and Gentlemen of the New England
Dry Goods Association: — [1]

THE proposed merger presents for the decision
of the people of Massachusetts the most important question which has arisen in this Commonwealth since the Civil War. I regret
deeply, therefore, that the eminent counsel of
the New York, New Haven and Hartford Railroad Company should have declined the invi-
tation of your association to present an argument in favor of the merger. His refusal to
discuss the question, following many like refusals of invitations extended by other associations to President Mellen and Vice-President
Byrnes, is obviously in pursuance of a definite
policy, and the policy appears to be this:
Having actually acquired the large block of
stock in the Boston and Maine Railroad secretly
and without authority under the laws of Massachusetts — "the less said about it, the better."

---

[1] An address delivered before the New England Dry Goods Association at Boston, February 11, 1908.

Against this Standard Oil policy of "Secrecy and Silence," the opponents of the merger vigorously protest.

Let us define what the merger question really is, and recall the circumstances under which it has arisen in Massachusetts.

The merger question is this: Shall the New York, New Haven and Hartford Railroad Company be permitted to acquire, through control of the Boston and Maine, a substantial monopoly of all transportation within New England and from New England to the South and West — a monopoly including alike steam railroads, trolleys and steamboat lines?

The circumstances under which this question arises are as follows:

For more than a generation the statutes of Massachusetts have declared that no railroad company shall acquire the stock of any other railroad company or of any street railway company without the express authority of our legislature. This has been the law of Massachusetts during all the time that the New York, New Haven and Hartford has operated any railroad in this Commonwealth.

THE NEW HAVEN DEFIANCE OF MASSACHUSETTS LAWS

With this law on the statute books, the New Haven Company, without seeking permission from our legislature, acquired within three years prior to June, 1906, nearly five hundred miles of trolleys in central and western Massachusetts. These trolley purchases threatened to extend into the Boston and Maine territory. The Boston and Maine had carefully obeyed the Massachusetts law which prohibited it from making trolley purchases; and it sought in 1905 authority from our legislature to do with the legislature's permission what the New Haven undertook to do in spite of legislative prohibition. The proposed change in the long-established policy of the Commonwealth was strenuously opposed. The question was referred to the Recess Committee of the legislature of 1905; and the question was again considered by the legislature of 1906, which refused to grant the permission asked.

Governor Guild then called attention to the situation in a memorable special message to the legislature (June 23, 1906) in which he said:

"I congratulate you on the defeat of a measure that would have sanctioned the possible consolidation of

all transportation in Massachusetts under the control
of a single corporation. The present railroad situation, however, is most unjust and inequitable. Our
steam railroad system is forbidden to meet the competition of electric street car lines by purchase or
control of their stock, but another controlled by men
who are not citizens of Massachusetts is not only
permitted to exercise that privilege, but is exerting
it to-day to such an extent that healthy competition
in western Massachusetts is already throttled.

"Slowly, surely, the control of our own railroads,
the control of the passage to market of every Massachusetts product, the control of the transportation
to and from his work of every Massachusetts citizen
is passing from our hands to those of aliens.

"I therefore urge upon you with all the strength
that is in me the passage of some legislation giving
relief from this grave injustice. Let Massachusetts
announce that transportation within her borders is
in the future to be controlled by the people of Massachusetts, and not by men beyond the reach of her
law and the inspiration of her ideals."

The message was immediately referred to the
Joint Committee on Railroads and Street
Railways. It was then late in June. The ses-
sion had already lasted nearly six months. All
other legislative business had been disposed of.
It was urged that consideration of a subject
so important should not then be entered upon.
The New Haven Company insisted that it had

no intention of violating the laws of Massachusetts; that it had been advised that, while the Massachusetts statute controlled Massachusetts corporations, like the Boston and Maine, the New Haven Company, having a Connecticut charter and operating through a subsidiary company, could legally purchase railroads and street railways in this State, regardless of the prohibition contained in the Massachusetts statute. It invited the Attorney General to bring proceedings to test the legal validity of its action. The New Haven Company asserted, furthermore, that it had no intent or desire to act contrary to what Massachusetts might declare to be its own policy in this respect.

THE NEW HAVEN BREACH OF FAITH

It was naturally suggested that this attitude on the part of the New Haven was assumed in order to delay legislation, so that meanwhile it might have the opportunity of continuing unhampered its purchases of Massachusetts properties. To meet this objection the following assurance was given to the legislative committee by the counsel of the New Haven Company:

JUNE 27, 1906.

REPRESENTATIVE JOSEPH WALKER, ESQ.

My Dear Mr. Walker: —

I have communicated with Mr. Mellen by telephone and got from him the following:

"Mr. Mellen authorizes Mr. Choate to state to the Legislature that he will not enter upon further acquisitions in Massachusetts other than those already contracted for, or build any trolley lines except such as are now under actual construction, until such time as the merger question has been settled.

"Mr. Mellen is willing, if the Committee desires it, to furnish a list of properties already contracted for or under construction, to avoid any future misunderstanding."

Yours truly,

(Signed)   CHARLES F. CHOATE, JR.

The list of Massachusetts trolley properties in which the New Haven was then interested was asked for and was furnished by Mr. Mellen. After that the legislature refused to pass any act dealing with this subject, and adjourned. Proceedings were then begun by the Attorney General to test the validity of the New Haven's position. While these proceedings were pending, the New Haven Company, regardless of the promise which had been given by Mr. Mellen on its behalf, proceeded with its purchases of Massachusetts trolleys. It bought the Milford, Attleborough, and Woonsocket Street

Railway Company; it bought the Hartford and Worcester, the Uxbridge and Blackstone and the Worcester and Holden Street Railway Companies. It acquired still other Massachusetts trackage through the Providence Securities Company.

And it did more. It acquired, without application to the legislature, and without notice in any way to the public, a large block of stock of the Boston and Maine Railroad — 109,948 shares out of a total of 295,096 outstanding in the hands of the public.

The great merger issue, the most important question which has arisen in Massachusetts in more than a generation, is thus brought before us by conduct on the part of the New Haven, which is not only in defiance of the settled policy of Massachusetts, as expressed in its statute law, but in defiance also of the promise solemnly given to the legislature of the Commonwealth and relied upon by it.

THE PROPOSED TRANSPORTATION MONOPOLY

Now, let us pass to the question of the merger itself and what it involves:

The possible advantages of a merger have not been made clear; but the objections, I submit, are clear, and they are insuperable.

First. The merger would result inevitably in a complete monopoly of transportation in New England.

It would mean control by the New Haven, not only of the Boston and Maine and the Maine Central systems, but of all railroads extending into New England, except the Grand Trunk and the Canadian Pacific. Outside the New Haven, the Boston and Maine and the Canadian systems, there is now no important railroad in New England, except the Boston and Albany and the Bangor and Aroostook. The Boston and Albany is already closely allied with the New Haven through a traffic arrangement. It will inevitably fall into the New Haven's grasp if the Boston and Maine does. So also will the Bangor and Aroostook and the small outlying roads.

But the merger means far more than a monopoly of the railroads. The New Haven has pursued relentlessly in each community to which its railroads extend the policy of suppressing all competition whatsoever, existing or potential — suppressing, at whatever cost, the competition not only of railroads but of steamship lines and of trolley lines as well. What it has already done in Connecticut and Rhode Island would inevitably be repeated in Massachusetts and in northern New England.

See how the New Haven has suppressed all competition between Boston and New York:

The New York and New England Railroad was designed to give us an independent all-rail line to New York. The New Haven induced the Connecticut legislature to refuse authority to construct the missing link. The New York and New England, however, actually gave us an independent rail and water line to New York *via* Norwich and a freight line *via* the Hudson River. The New York and New England passed into the hands of receivers and was purchased by the New Haven.

The Central New England Railroad intended (in connection with the Boston and Albany) to give us an independent line to the Pennsylvania coal fields, and another freight line to New York *via* the Hudson River. It met persistent obstruction in the legislature and in the courts of Connecticut. Its securities suffered, and it passed into the control of the New Haven.

A few years ago we had four rail and water lines to New York *via* the Sound — the Fall River Line, the Providence Line, the Stonington Line and the Norwich Line. All of these have passed into the hands of the New Haven; and another rail and water line to New York — the New Bedford Line — belongs also to the

New Haven.   Later a new competitor — the
Joy Line — arose; but soon it also passed into
New Haven control.

Finally the Enterprise Transportation Company was started, with boats running from
New York to Fall River and to Providence, and
with good promise of success.   The New Haven,
under secret cover of the Neptune Line and of
the Joy Line, entered into fierce competition
with the Enterprise Transportation Company.
Last October the Enterprise Transportation
Company succumbed.   It passed into the hands
of a receiver, and shortly after the New Haven
purchased the *Kennebec*, one of its best boats.

Not a single independent line of steamboats
exists between Massachusetts and New York
except the Metropolitan Line; and now that,
like other competitors of the New Haven, has
passed into receivers' hands.   May we not
expect to see, as the next step, its fine steamships, the *Harvard* and the *Yale*, flying the
New Haven flag, and the last vestige of
steamship competition disappear?

A few years ago we heard promises of independent trolley lines from Boston to New York.
The key to such a line was a franchise east
from New York City.   Two franchises were
given — the New York, Westchester, and Bos-

ton Railway Company and the New York and Port Chester Railroad Company — both given with the understanding that they should provide competition with the New Haven. The New Haven, at huge expense, acquired both franchises, and suppressed the nascent competition.

The policy of suppressing competition at any cost, pursued with respect to through lines between Boston and New York, has been followed by the New Haven throughout its territory. Under that policy the New Haven has acquired in all about fifteen hundred miles of trolley tracks — substantially all the trolleys in Connecticut and in Rhode Island, and nearly six hundred miles of line in central and western Massachusetts. It has even extended its lines into Vermont and northern New York.

No competitor was too large to be overcome, and none so insignificant as to be tolerated. Thus the New Haven acquired the lesser steamboat lines from New York to Connecticut and to Rhode Island ports — the Bridgeport Line, the New Haven Line, the Hartford Line and the Block Island Line. And with this nearer field covered, it undertook to extend its acquisitions to more distant ports, far beyond the present territory of its rail lines. It purchased, at large cost, a line from New York to Portland, Maine. It purchased a line from Boston to Philadelphia; and then, in connection with that purchase, it acquired a substantially controlling interest in the Merchants & Miners Transportation Company, with lines from Boston to Philadelphia, to Baltimore and to Norfolk.

If the New Haven secures the Boston and Maine system, it appears inevitable that the control which the New Haven has already acquired over the Boston and Albany through a traffic agreement will become practically absolute, that the New Haven's policy of acquiring trolleys will be further extended, and that soon all means of transportation by steam, by trolleys or by established steamship lines within New England, or from New England south and west, will be absolutely under New Haven control. The only other outlet for the people and products of Massachusetts will be across the Atlantic or to Canada.

AN ALIEN MONOPOLY

Second. This monopoly by the New Haven in transportation within New England and from New England south and west would be controlled by persons alien to Massachusetts, not only in their financial interests, but in their traditions and aspirations. How little the voice of Massachusetts would be heeded in the management may be inferred from the present conditions.

Although more than one-half of the stockholders of the New Haven are residents of Massachusetts, and although they owned, June 30, 1907, $35,000,000 out of $97,000,000 of New Haven stock outstanding in the hands of the public, as well as a larger part of its outstanding bonds and notes, Massachusetts has to-day upon the board of directors of the New Haven only two members out of twenty-three. It had one other member, making up the full board of twenty-four, but Mr. Charles F. Choate, long a member of the New Haven board, resigned recently.

Apparently the influence of the Massachusetts members in the board has been proportionate to their number.

ALIEN INTERESTS

Third. This monopoly in transportation would not only be controlled by non-residents of Massachusetts, but, as the New Haven's transportation lines would extend into at least six other States, the management, though intending to act with entire fairness to Massachusetts, might deem it proper to postpone the interests of Massachusetts to those of some other State or States. It might seem best to the management of this transportation monopoly to favor New York, or New London, or Providence, or Portland, as against Boston, not from any malevolent motive, but solely in the supposed interests of the company.

Yet we of Massachusetts have the solemn obligation of protecting and advancing our own welfare. We must not intrust the determination as to what our welfare demands to the decision of persons who may be influenced by considerations other than the interests of Massachusetts.

COMBINATION INEFFICIENT

Fourth. The very size of the proposed consolidated system and the diversity of its interests would be such as to impair its efficiency. The company would not be merely a large railroad company, but an aggregation of trolley companies, of steamship companies, of gas companies and power companies, an electric light company and a water-supply company. For thus comprehensive are the varying activities of the New Haven.

For every business concern there must be a

limit of greatest efficiency. What that limit is differs under varying conditions; but it is clear that an organization may be too large for efficient and economical management, as well as too small. The disadvantages attendant upon size may outweigh the advantages. Man's works have outgrown the capacity of the individual man. No matter what the organization, the capacity of the individual man must determine the success of a particular enterprise, not only financially to the owners, but in service to the community. Organization can do much to make possible larger efficient concerns; but organization can never be a substitute for initiative and for judgment. These must be supplied by the chief executive officers, and nature sets a limit to their possible accomplishment. Any transportation system which is called upon not merely to operate, but to develop its facilities, makes heavy demands upon its executive officers for initiative and for the exercise of sound judgment. And New England needs most emphatically development of its transportation facilities. To aid in this development we need more minds, not less.

Massachusetts has had and is having a lesson on the evils of too large units which should not readily be overlooked, namely the wretched service of the Boston and Albany Railroad. Even in mere operation that railroad has failed egregiously as compared with its condition prior to its lease to the New York Central. And what is the cause of this failure? Not, I submit, intentional neglect, on the part of the officials of the New York Central, of the interest of Massachusetts or the comfort of its patrons; not any purpose on the part of the management to prefer other communities to our own. The wretched service is due, in the main at least, to the fact that the New York Central System is greater than the administrative capacity of its executive officers. From that overgrowth its finances, its service and its patrons have alike suffered. And we may be sure that if we spread the ability of the New Haven management over a larger field we shall get, not better, but worse, service throughout the whole territory.

POLITICAL DANGERS

Fifth. The political dangers surrounding a monster corporation controlling all transportation facilities of New England are too obvious to require comment, particularly in the case of a corporation having the political traditions which surround the New Haven.

IMPOSSIBLE TO "SAFEGUARD" MONOPOLY

Sixth. It has been suggested that we accept the proposed monopoly in transportation, but provide safeguards.

This would be like surrendering liberty and substituting despotism with safeguards. There is no way in which to safeguard people from despotism except to prevent despotism. There is no way to safeguard the people from the evils of a private transportation monopoly except to prevent the monopoly. The objections to despotism and to monopoly are fundamental in human nature. They rest upon the innate and ineradicable selfishness of man. They rest upon the fact that absolute power inevitably leads to abuse. They rest upon the fact that progress flows only from struggle.

Furthermore, the most carefully devised safeguards are in many respects futile. The legislation authorizing the Boston and Albany lease was surrounded by all safeguards which an able governor, the legislature and our business organizations could devise. Have these safeguarding provisions reduced or made more tolerable the wretched service which we have received?

FALSE ANALOGY OF SOME LOCAL MONOPOLIES

Seventh. The analogy sometimes urged in favor of existing well-operated local monopolies in lighting, or gas, or street railways is delusive. In the first place a local gas company may have a monopoly of gas, but it has not a monopoly of lighting. It has the competition of electric light and the competition of oil.

But there is furthermore this marked difference: A local monopoly, like a gas company, or an electric light company or a street railway company, is but a creature, a servant of the State, wholly subject to the control of the State within which it is situated, wholly dependent for its prosperity upon the particular community which it serves; and in Massachusetts subject at all times to being terminated by the authority which created it.

The street railways of Massachusetts and the gas and electric light companies of Massachusetts, so far as they are monopolies, are performing practically, as agents of the State, public functions during good behavior. If they do not properly serve the community, the community may at any time terminate their franchises without even paying compensation. The right to run street railways in our public streets, the right to lay gas pipes or electric light wires, is a license merely, and is subject at all times to termination by the State and the municipal authorities.   There is no resemblance between such a monopoly of service covering a specific agency and the proposed New Haven monopoly of all transportation, a monopoly which claims rights under the laws of other States, and has asserted, though operating also in Massachusetts, that it is free from the restrictions imposed by the Massachusetts law.   And yet even in respect to these local service monopolies, Massachusetts recognized as early as 1894 that legislation was necessary to protect our people from the abuses incident to their being controlled by foreign corporations.

THE DANGERS OF A HOLDING COMPANY

Eighth.   Furthermore, it must be remembered that the New Haven Company is not a transportation company merely.   It is a huge holding company.   Its freedom in the issue of its own securities and its broad charter powers to hold securities of other companies expose us to the same conditions which have made Harriman a menace to America.   The primal cause of Harriman's power has been his ability to use the treasury and credit of the Union Pacific for practically any purpose. The Union Pacific was once a corporation with power to construct and operate a railroad within given limits. It has become a corporation with almost universal powers. And these large powers have been exercised practically by one individual, instead of being subject to the action of the stockholders.

Precisely similar operations may be pursued by the New Haven management, particularly since it secured its new Connecticut charter. Indeed its act in taking over this large interest in the Boston and Maine stock without action on the part of its own stockholders shows the extraordinary power heretofore exercised by the New Haven management. And the position for the future is even more dangerous than it has been in the past.

THE NEW HAVEN'S FINANCIAL CONDITION

Ninth. The above objections to the merger would exist even if the New Haven were to-day the financially strong and conservatively managed railroad which it was for many years prior to the advent of Mr. Mellen. But its financial condition is vastly changed. Once financially the strongest railroad company in America, it has by excessive expansion become perilously weak. The burdens which it has assumed must for many years greatly hamper its ability to serve the Commonwealth. Its impaired credit will prevent it from making further large improvements. The excessive prices paid to suppress trolley and steamboat competition create a permanent heavy charge upon all future traffic. How it will be able to bear the burdens thus created will, for some time, remain a question. But it is clear that the burdens already assumed have taxed to the uttermost, not only the ability of the managers, but the financial resources of the company itself. There is no surplus of ability or of credit which is available for extending its operations to another great system with a railroad mileage larger than its own.[1]

THE BOSTON AND MAINE

Tenth. And the Boston and Maine system is a great system. Its physical condition ought undoubtedly to be much improved. Additional facilities should be added and developed. But it possesses a solid foundation upon which to rest such development. The Boston and Maine is one of America's leading railroad systems. Including leased lines and railroads controlled

[1] This subject was discussed elaborately by Mr. Brandeis in a pamphlet entitled: "Financial Condition of the New York, New Haven & Hartford Railroad Company and of the Boston and Maine Railroad," published in December, 1907.

but operated separately, it has 3,559.52 miles
of line, and a total trackage of 5,817.71 miles.
For the year ending June 30, 1907, the gross
earnings of the system from operation were
$50,986,553.60. Of the 852 operating com-
panies in the United States, with an aggregate
mileage of 220,028 miles, reporting to the
Interstate Commerce Commission for the year
ending June 30, 1906, only thirteen had gross
earnings as large as that.

The miles of line owned or leased by the
Boston and Maine Railroad are 2,232.25 as
compared with 2,006.23 owned and leased by
the New Haven. The freight tonnage carried
one mile on these lines by the Boston and Maine
Railroad in the year ending June 30, 1907, was
2,296,970,964 as compared with 1,927,686,950
tons carried by the New Haven.

In the six years ending June 30, 1907, it increased its gross earnings 34.41 per cent, while
the increase of its capitalization was only 21.4
per cent, and the fixed charges increased only
2.72 per cent.

It is for Massachusetts to build up this distinctly Massachusetts railroad so that it shall
be worthy of Massachusetts; and the capital
required for making it meet all the demands of
Massachusetts for proper transportation facili-

ties can be and should be had. Massachusetts now recognizes the serious error which it committed in leasing the Boston and Albany to the New York Central. It should not commit the infinitely greater mistake of surrendering the Boston and Maine and its own prosperity to the New Haven Company.

IMMEDIATE LEGISLATION NECESSARY

Eleventh. The public did not discover until May, 1907, that the New Haven Company had secretly acquired this large block of stock in the Boston and Maine Railroad. It was then too late in the legislative session adequately and definitely to consider the subject. The legislature, with a view to providing for such consideration, passed a temporary restraining act by which the New Haven was prohibited until July 1, 1908, from attempting to vote on stock already acquired, or otherwise exercising control over the Boston and Maine Railroad, and from acquiring any additional stock in that company.

As this act expires July 1, 1908, and the New Haven Company, through the possession of nearly forty per cent of the Boston and Maine stock, has an interest so large that it may easily be converted into a working majority, the merger of the two systems will be practically complete on July 1, 1908, unless at the present session further legislation is enacted which shall not only compel the New Haven Company to dispose of the stock already acquired by it without authority under the laws of Massachusetts, but shall also prohibit it from in any way undertaking to exercise control over the Boston and Maine Railroad.

The control by the New Haven of the Boston and Maine through stock ownership would be the most dangerous form of merger — a merger with full power and with no responsibility.

Governor Guild wisely said:

"I therefore urge upon you with all the strength that is in me the passage of some legislation giving relief from this grave injustice. Let Massachusetts announce that transportation within her borders is in the future to be controlled by the people of Massachusetts, and not by men beyond the reach of her law and the inspiration of her ideals."

THE NEW HAVEN—AN UNREGULATED MONOPOLY [1]

THE breakdown of transportation in New England under the New Haven monopoly has become obvious. Demoralized and curtailed freight service, antiquated equipment, frequent wrecks, discontented employees, heavy depreciation in the market value of securities, and huge borrowing on short-time notes at high interest are the accumulated evidences of that deterioration in our transportation system which has been in process during the past eight years of aggressive monopolization.

The demand for a remedy is loud and urgent. What remedy shall we apply? Shall the monopoly now breaking down be broken up, or shall we attempt to patch it up by regulation?

Let us consider first the causes of our present ills.

These ills result from monopoly. But, while the policy of monopoly is the fundamental cause

[1] Published in the "Boston Journal," December 13, 1912.

of the deterioration of our transportation system, it has itself bred subsidiary causes; and of these subsidiary causes excessive bigness is probably the most potent.

Excessive bigness often attends monopoly; but the evils of excessive bigness are something distinct from and additional to the evils of monopoly. A business may be too big to be efficient without being a monopoly; and it may be a monopoly and yet (so far as concerns size) may be well within the limits of efficiency. Unfortunately, the so-called New Haven system suffers from both excessive bigness and from monopoly.

THE MONOPOLY

The New Haven monopoly of transportation in New England, now substantially complete, rests upon ownership or legal control of an effective interest in:

First. Substantially all the railroads in Maine, New Hampshire, Massachusetts, Rhode Island and Connecticut, except the Grand Trunk's line from Canada to New London and to Portland, the Canadian Pacific Line through northern Maine, and the Bangor and Aroostook.

Second. Substantially all the trolley lines in Rhode Island and Connecticut, the most important in western and central Massachusetts, and some in Maine, New Hampshire, Vermont and New York.

Third. Substantially all the steamship lines from any of the New England States to New York or Philadelphia or Baltimore.

The control which the New Haven, a privately owned corporation, holds over Boston is without parallel in the whole world. All railroads entering Boston (unless the Boston, Revere Beach and Lynn be called a railroad and is independent) are either owned by the New Haven, or controlled legally or through an effective interest; for it has such a partnership interest also in the Boston and Albany. All the coastwise steamship lines sailing from Boston for New York, Philadelphia or Baltimore are owned or controlled legally or influenced through an effective interest.

Among the American cities Boston ranks second in assessed wealth. Among the American seaports Boston ranks second in foreign commerce. Among the American centers of population Boston (including suburbs) ranks fourth. But Boston, alone of all the large cities of the United States, is in the grip of a railroad monopoly. The following is the position of the other large cities:

RAILROAD SYSTEMS

New York has	8	Milwaukee has	5
Chicago has	19	Cincinnati has	6
Philadelphia has	3	Newark has	5
St. Louis has	17	New Orleans has	5
Cleveland has	5	Minneapolis has	8
Baltimore has	3	Kansas City has	10
Pittsburg has	5	Louisville has	7
Detroit has	7	Denver has	6
Buffalo has	9	Seattle has	5
San Francisco has	4		

One railroad system has Boston

A DELUSIVE COMPARISON

Advocates of monopoly urge that the days of competition are passed; that to insist upon competition is to go backward, not forward; that (at least as to railroads and our public-service corporations) the path of progress lies in regulation, and that this remedy should be relied upon with respect to the New Haven.

The contention rests upon a half-truth and a misconception. Undoubtedly we need effective regulation of railroads as well as of other public-service corporations, whether they be monopolies or competitive concerns.

Undoubtedly, also, certain public services, local in character, like those supplying gas or water, will, on the whole, be best performed by monopolies, if effectively regulated; or, as in the case of the telephone, may as monopolies best serve the public convenience. But the instances of desirable private monopolies are exceptional; and the transportation service (other than local) is not within the exception. The difference is clearer.

1. When a local gas company (as in Boston) is given a monopoly, it is a monopoly only in gas, and not a monopoly in all lighting. The gas company is subjected to the competition of electric light and to the competition of oil.

Indeed, where a monopoly in gas and electric lighting is combined in the same company, the results are clearly less satisfactory than they are where the gas company and the electric light company compete vigorously (as in Boston) with one another.

2. There is also this marked difference between such a local monopoly, even if complete, and a monopoly like the New Haven:

A local monopoly, like a gas company or electric light company or a street railway company, is but a creature, a servant of the State, and as such wholly subject to the control of the State within which it is situated.

In Massachusetts, where such local monopolies have been satisfactorily conducted, the company has at all times been absolutely subject to the will, not only of the State, but even largely to the will of the particular community which it serves.

Its whole business is dependent upon the license to use the streets; and this license is terminable at the will of the people. In other words, the street railways of Massachusetts and the gas and electric light companies of Massachusetts are practically permitted to perform as agents of the State public functions during good behavior.

If they do not properly serve the community, the community may at any time terminate their franchises or license without even paying compensation.

Furthermore, these Massachusetts public-service corporations cannot issue any securities without the consent of the Commonwealth. They cannot pass under the control of a foreign corporation without their charter becoming liable to forfeiture. The control of the State is absolute.

This reserved power in the community is an effective weapon by which the community may compel the corporation to supply the service it needs. Thus it compelled the West End Street Railway to lease the Tremont Street subway and to remove the surface tracks from Tremont Street. It compelled the Boston Elevated to lease the line beyond Forest Hills and give five-cent

fare to Boston.   It compelled recently the consolidation of the West End and Elevated and
the leasing of the Boylston Street and Dorches-
ter subways.   Eighty-cent gas and the recent
satisfactory gas service were obtained by a like
struggle and the threat of municipal gas as an
alternative.

THE NEW HAVEN SUPERIOR TO OUR LAW

Between a street railway, gas or electric light
monopoly, existing under such conditions, and
the New Haven monopoly in transportation
there is no real resemblance.   The New Haven
claims rights under the laws of seven States and,
in addition, under acts of Congress.   Massachusetts has, except in strictly local matters,
no effective legal control over the company.
Neither the Massachusetts legislature, nor any
commission it may create, can regulate the
New Haven in any of its important functions.
Any statute attempting to do so would be void
as interfering with interstate commerce.

And Massachusetts cannot enforce her will
even as to intrastate matters, as it does in the
case of street railways, gas and other street-using
corporations; because the railroad franchises
cannot be taken without paying compensation.
Massachusetts prohibited the New Haven from

issuing stock without the consent of the railroad commissioners. The New Haven disobeyed the laws with impunity. Massachusetts laws prohibited the New Haven from issuing more bonds than stock. The New Haven disobeyed the laws with impunity. Massachusetts laws prohibited the New Haven from acquiring steamship lines. The New Haven disobeyed the laws with impunity. Massachusetts laws prohibited the New Haven from consolidating with other companies. The New Haven disobeyed the laws with impunity. In each instance these prohibitions were a part of Massachusetts' plan for regulating railroad companies; but the New Haven claimed the right to act under the laws of another State, and successfully defied Massachusetts.

And the recent Grand Trunk incident furnished another and a striking instance of our inability to regulate this monopoly. The New Haven, having been unable to prevent the passing of the enabling act providing for this competition, nullified the law by an arrangement with the Grand Trunk.

A DIVIDED LOYALTY

There is, however, another and very important respect in which local monopolies, like gas and electric light and street railways, differ from the interstate monopolies. The prosperity of the local monopoly is absolutely dependent upon the prosperity of the community in which it is situated. Self-interest demands that the company owning the local monopoly should endeavor to advance the prosperity of the community which it serves. But in the case of the New Haven monopoly there are several communities served and there is a distinct diversity of interest between those communities. The interests of Boston and northern New England are in many respects directly opposed to the interests of New York City. The interests of our merchants and manufacturers are in many respects directly opposed to the interests of the Wall Street financiers, who control the destinies of the New Haven. Northern New England might suffer by the New Haven serving New York, Connecticut and Rhode Island in preference to this Commonwealth. The prosperity of Massachusetts and northern New England is at present absolutely dependent on the New Haven; but the New Haven's prosperity is not absolutely dependent upon Massachusetts and northern New England.

THE LIMITS OF REGULATION

The policy of regulating public-service companies is sound; but it must not be over-worked. The scope of any possible effective regulation of an interstate railroad, either by the federal or by State commissions, is limited to a relatively narrow sphere. Regulation may prevent positive abuses, like discriminations, or rebating, or excessive rates. Regulation may prevent persistent disregard of definite public demands, like that for specific trains or for stops at certain stations. Regulation may compel the correction of definite evils, like the use of unsanitary cars. But regulation cannot make an inefficient business efficient. Regulation cannot convert a poorly managed railroad into a well-managed railroad. Regulation cannot supply initiative or energy. Regulation cannot infuse into railroad executives the will to please the people. Regulation cannot overcome the anæmia or wasting-sickness which attends monopoly. Regulation may curb, but it cannot develop the action of railroad officials.

For no commission, however broad its powers, however able, fearless and diligent its members, can perform the functions of general manager and the board of directors of a railroad sys-

tem; or supply the incentive and the eagerness
to please the public and that development which
results from the necessities of competition.
It is to lack of efficiency, to the lack of appreciation of the community's needs, and to the
lack of this eagerness to please its customers
that our demoralized transportation service is
in large measure due.

For instance, bad freight service has seriously
impaired the prosperity of New England. Deliveries of freight have been almost incredibly
slow and unreliable. The effect upon the business concerns has been very serious. Success of
individual businesses has been imperilled. Prosperity of all New England has been retarded.
All this has happened in a period in which the
country has been blessed with an able, fearless and upright Interstate Commerce Commission, possessing broad legal powers. The recent
hearings before that commission have disclosed
the evils from which the community suffers.
The recent public disclosures will undoubtedly result in correcting some specific evils
which have been pointed out; but the commission cannot by any order make the railroads
give the shippers good service. Regulation
cannot produce efficient and enlightened railroad operation in the interests of the public;

and without that the community cannot get satisfactory service.

The efficiency of regulation, even within its acknowledged sphere, is quite limited. The Bridgeport wreck of 1911 was caused, as the Interstate Commerce Commission found, by the maintenance of a short crossover. It was undoubtedly lack of judgment in the railroad originally to establish such a short crossover. When the short crossover was found to be the cause of the accident, the commission recommended its abolition. The recommendation was ignored by the railroad; the change was not made. And the terrible Westport accident of 1912 was the result of ignoring the recommendation. The Interstate Commerce Commission surely performed its full duty of regulation in this connection; and yet the community was subjected to this serious result of inefficiency in railroading.

THE NEED OF COMPETITION

No one has recognized more fully than members of the Interstate Commerce Commission the limitation of accomplishment through railroad regulation. No one recognizes better than they the continuing need of competition to secure satisfactory service.

This appears very clearly from Chairman Prouty's letter to the President, written March 12, 1912, referring to the proposal to permit railroad-owned ships to use the Panama Canal, but referring generally to all water transportation, in which he says:

"The commission, after consideration, is unanimously of the opinion that if the waterways of this country are to be of any substantial benefit in the way of reducing the rates of transportation, it is absolutely essential that rail carriers be prohibited from owning or controlling, directly or indirectly, competing water carriers."

Congress, also, by an overwhelming majority, testified to its conviction that the Interstate Commerce Commission was right in declaring such competition in transportation to be essential to our prosperity; for it not only prohibited railroad-owned steamships from using the Panama Canal, but insisted upon inserting in the Canal Act a general provision by which all railroads engaged in interstate commerce are prohibited from owning or operating any competing water lines on any routes after July 1, 1914, unless the commission should, upon investigation of the particular line, find that its operation is of advantage to the convenience and commerce of the people; or that such service would not retard competition by other vessels on the water route under consideration.

Of course, competition between carriers is not synonymous with rate-cutting. New England longs for good service even more than for lower rates. The Interstate Commerce Commission may effectively prevent increases in rates; and may protect the community by enforcing reductions.

But even in its admitted field care must always be taken not to overwork the Interstate Commerce Commission by creating conditions of monopoly under which burdens would develop greater than it could probably bear. The excellent work which the Commission has so far done has been possible only because existing competition between railroads has to a large extent produced development and supply of reasonable facilities, and, in the main, reasonable rates; each railroad acting, to a certain extent, as a check upon the other. Such is the condition in Wisconsin, where the best success in regulation of railroads has been attained. To abandon competition in transportation and rely upon regulation as a safeguard against the evils of monopoly would be like surrendering liberty and regulating despotism.

THE MONOPOLY UNCONTROLLABLE

The Grand Trunk incident shows clearly that a powerful interstate monopoly like the New Haven with its banking affiliations is uncontrollable, so long as the monopoly is allowed to continue. The people of Massachusetts and of Rhode Island, after some unsatisfactory experience with the New Haven's monopoly of transportation, determined to secure competition. The Boston Chamber of Commerce and other trade organizations of these States insisted that the Grand Trunk should be permitted to secure an independent entrance into Boston and into Providence. The governors of these sovereign States, the mayors of their chief cities, recommended the necessary legislation. The legislatures, after long deliberation, passed the required acts in spite of all the opposition which the New Haven could interpose. Construction of the line through Massachusetts to Providence was commenced, and, despite the obstacles presented by the New Haven, was nearing completion. Contracts were let for the new line of Grand Trunk boats from Providence to New York. Surveys for the Grand Trunk railroad into Boston were being made.

Then the powerful New Haven monopoly, by threat, bribe or other influence, stopped construction and secured the abandonment of the competitive project. The laws of Massachusetts and of Rhode Island were nullified; the will of the people of two supposedly sovereign States was defied; and there is no power of regulation now possessed by, or which can be conferred upon, any State railroad commission or the Interstate Commerce Commission which could prevent or redress such a wrong to the people.

THE CURSE OF BIGNESS

But even if it were possible to really regulate the New Haven monopoly, efficient and satisfactory transportation would be unattainable because the New Haven suffers not only from monopoly, but also from excessive bigness.

The New Haven is not strictly a system; it is an agglomeration of properties. Its huge bulk was attained, not by normal growth, but by acquisition. It represents not so much a development as a putting together. Furthermore, it is an agglomeration, not of railroads merely, but of railroads, steamships, trolleys and other properties.

Here are some of the properties which the New Haven railroad, with 2,006 miles of line, has purchased or acquired control of, or an effective interest in, during the last eight years of aggressive monopolization:

(1) RAILROADS	MILES OF LINE
Boston and Maine system	2,449
Montpelier and Wells River and the Barre railroads . .	66
Maine Central system	1,410
Sandy River and Rangeley Lakes	102
Bridgeton and Saco	21
Sebasticook and Moosehead	16
Rangeley Lakes and Megantic	11
New York, Ontario and Western	513
Central New England	272
New York, Westchester and Boston	274
	4,934

These railroads have a total of 7,245 miles of track.

The New Haven acquired also:

1. One-half the New York Central holdings of preferred stock (and would have acquired all but for adverse legal proceedings) in the Rutland Railroad, with 415 miles of line.

2. One-half interest in the results of operating the Boston and Albany, with 392 miles of line.

(2) TROLLEYS	MILES OF LINE
In Connecticut, 37 trolley lines	773
In Rhode Island, 12 trolleys	347
In Massachusetts, 19 trolley lines	481
(The New Haven claims to have divested itself of control of a large part of these.)	
In New York, 3 trolley lines	58
In New Hampshire, 2 trolley lines	47
In Vermont, 1 trolley line	21
	1,727

Joy Line.
Hartford and New York Transportation Company.
Maine Steamship Line (now merged in Eastern Steamship Company).
Metropolitan Steamship Company (now merged in Eastern Steamship Company).
Boston and Philadelphia (now merged in Merchants' and Miners').

To acquire the mere control or interest in new properties, the New Haven invested, during the last ten years of aggressive monopolization, about $250,000,000. In that period the New Haven increased its own capitalization and other direct and contingent liabilities nearly sixfold, or from $87,000,000 to $530,000,000.

Before the New Haven acquired control of these properties they were in large part operated independently and by different groups of executive officers. Since the acquisition, and as a necessary incident of incorporating them into the so-called system, a few New Haven officials have, in effect, been charged with the management of them all. For a few men to manage all these properties well surpasses human capacity.

INTENSIVE RAILROADING

The bulk of the New Haven properties is huge; but it is not the huge bulk alone which renders impossible the task of efficient management. The New Haven properties are diverse in character and widely scattered; but it is not these facts which present the most serious difficulty in their operation. The insuperable obstacle to efficient management of the New Haven properties, in addition to the status of monopoly, lies in the fact that almost each one of these many diverse properties, agglomerated into a so-called system, presents many problems which are not only important, but are individual to the particular property and to the particular community served by it. That results necessarily from the conditions surrounding transportation in New England.

For the solution of each of these problems there is required, not only separate investigation, but careful weighing of relevant facts. In order to secure unity of purpose and action, all these problems must be passed upon ultimately by the same chief executives. Now, the number of such decisions which any man can make, however able and hard-working he may be, and the extent of supervision which any man can effectively apply, are obviously very limited. Organization may accomplish much in extending the scope of work possible for an executive; but there is an obvious limit, also, to the efficacy of organization; for the success of the whole enterprise demands that the executive must be able to comprehend all the important facts bearing upon the properties. Real efficiency in any business in which conditions are ever changing must ultimately depend, in large measure, upon the correctness of judgment formed from day to day on the problems as they arise. And it is an essential of sound judgment that the executives have time to know and correlate the facts.

MERE CHANGE OF MANAGEMENT NO REMEDY

Men of good judgment must necessarily make many errors if they work under the conditions with which the high New Haven officials have been confronted during the past eight years. If the conditions remain the same, the New Haven cannot, by removing present officials and substituting others, escape from making similar errors in the future; nor can we aid the matter materially by regulation, state or federal. Present ills are due, in the main, to the fundamental error of adopting the policy of monopoly. The ills can be remedied only by abandoning that policy. Present conditions make bad management inevitable. Bad management of the New Haven can be avoided in the future only by changing the controlling conditions under which the properties are to be operated; and that involves reducing the so-called system to a size consistent with efficiency, and subjecting those who manage it to that constant incentive and education which come from having "to make good" in competitive business.

It has been urged that the so-called New Haven system is not too large; and some other large railroad systems have been referred to as evidence of this. It may be answered, in the first place, that none of those systems are monopolies; and that few of them own any trolleys and relatively few are operating steamship lines. Furthermore, several of them appear also to have exceeded the limit of greatest efficiency. But no comparison can properly be made between other large systems and the so-called New Haven system. With a few notable exceptions the size of most of the other systems was, in the main attained by gradual growth. Their main line was built, then extended, and branches were constructed in various directions in obedience largely to actual necessities of the States or of the railroads. Their problems were

important and were difficult; but as compared
with the problems arising from operation in New
England they were relatively few and simple.
In the West the same problem is repeated on
many parts of the line; there a general rule can
frequently be laid down. Here nearly every grave
problem is an individual one. New England
railroading is done in an old and settled community; the population is congested; and here,
to a certain extent, conditions became fixed
even before the days of railroading.

The great growth of population and of business
in New England has brought with it many problems, individual in character, but which are
nevertheless of a nature to require consideration
by the high executives. Indeed, this difference
between the railroad situation in other parts of
the country and that of the East has been frequently urged by the railroad officials themselves. Railroading, to be done efficiently and
prosperously in New England, must be done far
more intensively than in newer sections of the
country. New England railroading may, perhaps, be likened to our intensive market gar-
dening, or to tobacco growing in the Connecticut valley, in contrast to the big wheat farms of
the West.

ENDING OF MONOPOLY IMPERATIVE

Even if the size of the so-called New Haven system were much reduced, yet the efficient service demanded by the public could not be attained so long as a monopoly in transportation is permitted to exist. Competition, except in purely local traffic, subject to complete regulation as above described, should be introduced so far as possible everywhere. But, as above explained, this does not mean rate-cutting. Competition is not possible everywhere on the New Haven system; but a broad field of healthy competition is open to New England. Bordering largely on the Atlantic Ocean, blessed with fine harbors, we should have the full benefit of water competition and of the low rates which are consistent with reasonable profit to those engaged in water transportation. Being a thickly settled community, we should have the full benefit of competition through interurban electrics. The New Haven has robbed New England of the benefit both of water competition and of trolley competition.

In order to attain its transportation monopoly the New Haven bought up at huge cost not only competing railroads, but water and trolley lines. To secure satisfactory transpor-

tation conditions in New England, water and
trolley competition must be reëstablished.
Connecticut, Rhode Island and Massachusetts
should insist upon separate ownership of rail,
water and trolley lines, which are naturally
competitive.

But the establishment of competing water and
trolley lines would not afford complete relief.
Neither steamships nor trolleys could break the
monopoly in a large part of our traffic. To do
that railroad competition is essential. To this
end the Boston and Maine must be completely
separated from the New Haven. Such separation would reinstate important competition in
transportation within the State; and without
such separation adequate competition is unattainable in the most important interstate traffic;
for instance, to Chicago, St. Louis and the West.

Without establishing an important absolutely
independent railroad system in our community,
the New Haven and the community will be deprived of that opportunity of comparing standards of operation which is essential to the best
accomplishment in any department of business.

Unless the Boston and Maine is separated
from the New Haven, Massachusetts and
northern New England will be without a railroad system wholly devoted to its interests.

LAWS

The recent decision of the United States Supreme Court, holding the Union-Southern Pacific merger illegal, may lead the administration to bring proceedings to end this huge New Haven monopoly by reinstituting the proceedings commenced in 1908 by President Roosevelt and dismissed by the new administration in 1909, after the Boston Railroad Holding Company bill was passed. And so far as concerns the water lines, relief may also be afforded through the Interstate Commerce Commission under the provisions of the recent act of Congress.

But proper transportation conditions will probably not be secured unless the States also take appropriate action. The States can effect the separation of the trolley lines. Rhode Island seems inclined to acquire and complete the railroad line which the Grand Trunk was induced by the New Haven to abandon. And at present the most certain and expeditious method of securing the separation of the Boston and Maine from the New Haven appears to be for the Commonwealth of Massachusetts to exercise the right reserved to it in the Massachusetts act of 1909, incorporating the Boston

Railroad Holding Company (the New Haven's subsidiary which holds for it the Boston and Maine stock). That act provides:

"The Commonwealth may at any time, by act of the Legislature upon one year's notice, take or require the securities."

The New Haven is clearly bound by the provisions of this statute, as the act expressly provides:

"The acquisition by any railroad corporation . . . of any bonds, stocks, notes, or other evidence of indebtedness of said Boston Railroad Holding Company shall be deemed to be an acceptance by said railroad corporation of all the terms and provisions of this act."

The legislature of Massachusetts passed the holding company bill upon the assurance of Governor Draper and of the Attorney General that by so doing the Commonwealth would acquire potential control over the Boston and Maine. The aggressions of private monopoly compel it now to exercise this reserved power to take the stock. After the Commonwealth has acquired the stock, it may retain the same and assume the responsibility of a majority owner in a corporation to choose its managing officials; or it may transfer the stock under proper safeguards to others, who will operate it in the interest of Massachusetts and northern New England. But action by the State to take over the stock seems necessary now.

"A condition and not a theory confronts us."

AN AID TO RAILROAD EFFICIENCY[1]

THE decision of the Interstate Commerce Commission having established that there shall be no general advance in railroad freight rates, the attention of the public should now be directed toward encouraging improvements in service and in operating conditions and to the development of transportation facilities. To this end greater efficiency in management, and an ample supply of capital, are necessary.

Railroading being a private business, the corporations must, in order to secure capital as well as ability and zeal in management, offer the ordinary incentives incident to successful private businesses, namely, liberal money rewards. Capital or property will yield vastly differing returns according to the degree of judgment and efficiency applied in management. In order to secure efficient administration of railroads, we must make the rewards proportional to the efficiency. The establish-

[1] A statement before the (Hadley) Railroad Securities Commission, March 6, 1911: Published in "Engineering Magazine," October, 1911.

ment, therefore, of any rule fixing a maximum return on capital invested in railroads would tend to prevent efficiency by placing a limit on achievement.

To-day even though no fixed maximum return is definitely adopted, efficiency in management is in danger of being punished; whereas it should be rewarded. Efficiency is naturally reflected in large net earnings; and as no ready means exists for determining whether larger net earnings are due to greater efficiency in management or to higher rates, large earnings are frequently accepted as evidence that rates are too high and lead to demands for reduction; when, in fact, the large earnings may be due wholly to better management. To take from railroad corporations the natural fruits of efficiency — that is, greater money rewards — must create a sense of injustice suffered, which paralyzes effort, invites inefficiency and produces slip-shod management. The public interest, as well as justice, demands, therefore, the due appreciation of greater efficiency in management, and the granting of adequate rewards. In other words, private capital embarked in a quasi-public business ought to receive compensation on a sliding scale; so that the greater the service to the public, the greater the profit to those furnishing that service.

Boston applied the sliding-scale system to the production and sale of gas. There the dividend to the stockholders rises as the selling price to the public is reduced; and that system has proved eminently satisfactory both to the public and to the investor. The problem presented in the gas business was so simple that it was possible to apply the principle and make it operate automatically. The problem in railroading is infinitely more difficult, owing to the complexities arising from multitudinous rates, varying conditions and degrees of service and interstate relations. But if the principle of the sliding scale is once definitely recognized by the Interstate Commerce Commission, State railroad commissions and the people, as properly controlling the relations between the public and railroad corporations, methods will undoubtedly be worked out in time by which it can be safely applied.

The first step in applying the principle of the sliding scale must be, however, to devise means of determining degrees of efficiency, — and that involves determining the unit cost of each operation on each railroad. Unless costs are so ascertained, no true measure of efficiency can be arrived at. The knowledge that the average annual cost per locomotive for repairs, renewals and depreciation on one railroad is $3832.37 and on another is $2709.27 would be a very unsafe ground for determining the relative economy of operation on the two railroads. The conditions on the two railroads and the standards of renewal and depreciation may vary so greatly that the company expending the greater sum may actually have conducted its locomotive use and repair more economically and efficiently than the railroad expending less. We must reduce each operation to its ultimate unit and ascertain the cost of that before a proper basis of comparison can be secured. We must learn not merely the cost of turning a wheel of a standard size and character, the cost of laying a tie or a rail under standard conditions; but even these relatively simple operations must be again analyzed and separated into their component elements before a safe basis of relative costs can be arrived at.

The fact that railroads are subject in their accounting to the orders of the Interstate Commerce Commission makes it possible to require that each company should ascertain and report to the commission the ultimate unit costs of each operation in each department of the railroad. The further fact that the railroad business is largely non-competitive, makes it proper to publish these costs and to give to each railroad the benefit of knowing the lowest unit cost of each operation attained by any railroad and how it was attained.

To aid in this work the Interstate Commerce Commission should establish a Bureau of Railroad Costs by which the ascertainment of costs may be supervised and the results analyzed, classified and compared. Knowledge of the best methods would thus become the common property of railroad men. That alone would lead directly to great advances in efficiency and economy. But the adoption of the best existing methods would be merely the beginning of the great advance. The ascertainment of the lowest existing costs would inevitably be followed by widespread striving to eliminate further waste of time, effort and material and to find ever better methods. With the introduction of exact tests of efficiency, with the establishment of dependable standards of comparison, railroad operation would soon develop into a recognized profession; and those who pursue it would be stimulated like scientists and engineers to ever higher achievements.

There should be established also an Experiment Station in Railroad Efficiency. Such a station could be conducted similarly to the Agricultural experiment stations and the Office of Roads in the Department of Agriculture. The former has been potent in raising the standard in agriculture; the latter has advanced road-building throughout the United States. The coöperation of the government in furthering railroad efficiency would be no less effective. The Bureau would undoubtedly develop valuable inventions and discoveries in its own laboratories, as the various experiment stations of the Agricultural Department have done. But it would be of even greater service in testing the inventions made and methods suggested by others; and it could bring those of especial value to the attention of the railroads. Hundreds of inventions, hundreds of new methods which, if adopted, would enhance the efficiency of railroad operation, and introduce economies of wide scope, have remained unused, because they are not known to the operating men. Many of these inventions are not now in use merely because no single railroad was willing to give the time or incur the expense of testing their value; many because the inventor or discoverer was unable to secure a hearing or a fair test. There are undoubtedly also a large number of devices and methods in use in foreign countries of which our railway managers have either no knowledge or have but inadequate information.

It is a proper function of our government to make such investigations and to give to the railroads the benefit thereof. The railroads are the greatest single industry in the United States next to agriculture. The interest of the general public to secure efficient and economical transportation is so great that the government would be fully justified in incurring any reasonable expense to aid in increasing railroad efficiency. And in view of the obligations already assumed by the government in the regulation of railroad rates and service, it should proceed now to thus lend its aid to the railroads, securing to them greater justice by permitting them to enjoy earnings on capital in proportion to the efficiency of their management.

THE OPPORTUNITY IN THE LAW[1]

I ASSUME that in asking me to talk to you on the Ethics of the Legal Profession, you do not wish me to enter upon a discussion of the relation of law to morals, or to attempt to acquaint you with those detailed rules of ethics which lawyers have occasion to apply from day to day in their practice. What you want is this: Standing not far from the threshold of active life, feeling the generous impulse for service which the University fosters, you wish to know whether the legal profession would afford you special opportunities for usefulness to your fellow-men, and, if so, what the obligations and limitations are which it imposes. I say special opportunities, because every legitimate occupation, be it profession or business or trade, furnishes abundant opportunities for usefulness, if pursued in what Matthew Arnold called "the grand manner." It is, as a rule, far more important *how* men pursue their occupation than *what* the occupation is which they select.

[1] An address delivered May 4, 1905, at Phillips Brooks House, before the Harvard Ethical Society.

But the legal profession does afford in America unusual opportunities for usefulness. That this has been so in the past, no one acquainted with the history of our institutions can for a moment doubt. The great achievement of the English-speaking people is the attainment of liberty through law. It is natural, therefore, that those who have been trained in the law should have borne an important part in that struggle for liberty and in the government which resulted. Accordingly, we find that in America the lawyer was in the earlier period almost omnipresent in the State. Nearly every great lawyer was then a statesman; and nearly every statesman, great or small, was a lawyer. DeTocqueville, the first important foreign observer of American political institutions, said of the United States seventy-five years ago:

"In America there are no nobles or literary men, and the people are apt to mistrust the wealthy; lawyers, consequently, form the highest political class. . . . As the lawyers form the only enlightened class whom the people do not mistrust, they are naturally called upon to occupy most of the public stations. They fill the legislative assemblies and are at the head of the administration; they consequently exercise a powerful influence upon the formation of the law and upon its execution."

For centuries before the American Revolution the lawyer had played an important part in England. His importance in the State became much greater in America. One reason for this, as DeTocqueville indicated, was the fact that we possessed no class like the nobles, which took part in government through privilege. A more potent reason was that with the introduction of a written constitution the law became with us a far more important factor in the ordinary conduct of political life than it did in England. Legal questions were constantly arising and the lawyer was necessary to settle them. But I take it the paramount reason why the lawyer has played so large a part in our political life is that his training fits him especially to grapple with the questions which are presented in a democracy.

The whole training of the lawyer leads to the development of judgment. His early training— his work with books in the study of legal rules — teaches him patient research and develops both the memory and the reasoning faculties. He becomes practised in logic; and yet the use of the reasoning faculties in the study of law is very different from their use, say, in metaphysics. The lawyer's processes of reasoning, his logical conclusions, are being constantly tested by experience.   He is running up against facts at every point.   Indeed it is a maxim of the law: Out of the facts grows the law; that is, propositions are not considered abstractly, but always with reference to facts.

Furthermore, in the investigation of the facts the lawyer differs very materially from the scientist or the scholar. The lawyer's investigations into the facts are limited by time and space.   His investigations have reference always to some practical end. Unlike the scientist, he ordinarily cannot refuse to reach a conclusion on the ground that he lacks the facts sufficient to enable one to form an opinion. He must form an opinion from those facts which he has gathered; he must reason from the facts within his grasp.

If the lawyer's practice is a general one, his field of observation extends, in course of time, into almost every sphere of business and of life. The facts so gathered ripen his judgment. His memory is trained to retentiveness. His mind becomes practised in discrimination as well as in generalization. He is an observer of men even more than of things. He not only sees men of all kinds, but knows their deepest secrets; sees them in situations which "try men's souls." He is apt to become a good judge of men.

Then, contrary to what might seem to be the habit of the lawyer's mind, the practice of law tends to make the lawyer judicial in attitude and extremely tolerant. His profession rests upon the postulate that no contested question can be properly decided until both sides are heard. His experience teaches him that nearly every question has two sides; and very often he finds — after decision of judge or jury — that both he and his opponent were in the wrong. The practice of law creates thus a habit of mind, and leads to attainments which are distinctly different from those developed in most professions or outside of the professions. These are the reasons why the lawyer has acquired a position materially different from that of other men. It is the position of the adviser of men.

Your chairman said: "People have the impression to-day that the lawyer has become mercenary." It is true that the lawyer has become largely a part of the business world. Mr. Bryce said twenty years ago when he compared the America of 1885 with the America of DeTocqueville:

"Taking a general survey of the facts of to-day, as compared with the facts of sixty years ago, it is clear that the Bar counts for less as a guiding and restraining power, tempering the crudity or haste of democracy by its attachment to rule and precedent, than it did."

And in reviewing American conditions after his recent visit Mr. Bryce said:

"Lawyers are now to a greater extent than formerly business men, a part of the great organized system of industrial and financial enterprise. They are less than formerly the students of a particular kind of learning, the practitioners of a particular art. And they do not seem to be so much of a distinct professional class."

That statement was made by a very sympathetic observer of American institutions; but it is clear that Mr. Bryce coincides in the view commonly expressed, that the Bar had become commercialized through its connection with business. I am inclined to think that this view is not altogether correct. Probably business has become professionalized as much as the Bar has become commercialized. Is it not this which has made the lawyer so important a part of the business world?

The ordinary man thinks of the Bar as a body of men who are trying cases, perhaps even trying criminal cases. Of course there is an immense amount of litigation going on; and a great deal of the time of many lawyers is devoted to litigation. But by far the greater part of the work done by lawyers is done not in court, but in advising men on important matters, and mainly in business affairs. In guiding these affairs industrial and financial, lawyers are needed, not only because of the legal questions involved, but because the particular mental attributes and attainments which the legal profession develops are demanded in the proper handling of these large financial or industrial affairs. The magnitude and scope of these operations remove them almost wholly from the realm of "petty trafficking" which people formerly used to associate with trade. The questions which arise are more nearly questions of statesmanship. The relations created call in many instances for the exercise of the highest diplomacy. The magnitude, difficulty and importance of the problems involved are often as great as in the matters of state with which lawyers were formerly frequently associated. The questions appear in a different guise; but they are similar. The relations between rival railroad systems are like the relations between neighboring kingdoms. The relations of the great trusts to the consumers or to their employees is like that of feudal lords to commoners or dependents. The relations of public-service corporations to the people raise questions not unlike those presented by the monopolies of old.

So some of the ablest American lawyers of this generation, after acting as professional advisers of great corporations, have become finally their managers. The controlling intellect of the great Atchison Railroad System, its vice-president, Mr. Victor Morawetz, graduated at the Harvard Law School about twenty-five years ago, and shortly afterward attained distinction by writing an extraordinarily good book on the Law of Corporations. The head of the great Bell Telephone System of the United States, Mr. Frederick P. Fish, was at the time of his appointment to that office probably our leading patent lawyer. In the same way, and for the same reason, lawyers have entered into the world of finance. Mr. James J. Storrow, who was a law partner of Mr. Fish, has become a leading member of the old banking firm of Lee, Higginson & Co. A former law partner of Mr. Morawetz, Mr. Charles Steele, became a member of the firm of J. P. Morgan & Co. Their legal training was called for in the business world, because business has tended to become professionalized. And thus, although the lawyer is not playing in affairs of state the part he once did, his influence is, or at all events may be, quite as important as it ever was in the United States; and it is simply a question how that influence is to be exerted.

It is true that at the present time the lawyer does not hold as high a position with the people as he held seventy-five or indeed fifty years ago; but the reason is not lack of opportunity. It is this: Instead of holding a position of independence, between the wealthy and the people, prepared to curb the excesses of either, able lawyers have, to a large extent, allowed themselves to become adjuncts of great corporations and have neglected the obligation to use their powers for the protection of the people. We hear much of the "corporation lawyer," and far too little of the "people's lawyer." The great opportunity of the American Bar is and will be to stand again as it did in the past, ready to protect also the interests of the people.

Mr. Bryce, in discussing our Bar, said, in his "American Commonwealth":

"But I am bound to add that some judicious American observers hold that the last thirty years have witnessed a certain decadence in the Bar of the great cities. They say that the growth of the enormously rich and powerful corporations willing to pay vast sums for questionable services has seduced the virtue of some counsel whose eminence makes their example important."

The leading lawyers of the United States have been engaged mainly in supporting the claims of the corporations; often in endeavoring to evade or nullify the extremely crude laws by which legislators sought to regulate the power or curb the excesses of corporations.

Such questions as the regulation of trusts, the fixing of railway rates, the municipalization of public utilities, the relation between capital and labor, call for the exercise of legal ability of the highest order. Up to the present time the legal ability of a high order which has been expended on those questions has been almost wholly in opposition to the contentions of the people. The leaders of the Bar, without any preconceived intent on their part, and rather as an incident to their professional standing, have, with rare exceptions, been ranged on the side of the corporations, and the people have been represented, in the main, by men of very meagre legal ability.

If these problems are to be settled right, this condition cannot continue. Our country is, after all, not a country of dollars, but of ballots. The immense corporate wealth will necessarily develop a hostility from which much trouble will come to us unless the excesses of capital are curbed, through the respect for law, as the excesses of democracy were curbed seventy-five years ago. There will come a revolt of the people against the capitalists, unless the aspirations of the people are given some adequate legal expression; and to this end coöperation of the abler lawyers is essential.

For nearly a generation the leaders of the Bar have, with few exceptions, not only failed to take part in constructive legislation designed to solve in the public interest our great social, economic and industrial problems; but they have failed likewise to oppose legislation prompted by selfish interests. They have often gone further in disregard of common weal. They have often advocated, as lawyers, legislative measures which as citizens they could not approve, and have endeavored to justify themselves by a false analogy. They have erroneously assumed that the rule of ethics to be applied to a lawyer's advocacy is the same where he acts for private interests against the public, as it is in litigation between private individuals.

The ethical question which laymen most frequently ask about the legal profession is this: How can a lawyer take a case which he does not

believe in? The profession is regarded as necessarily somewhat immoral, because its members
are supposed to be habitually taking cases
of that character. As a practical matter,
the lawyer is not often harassed by this
problem; partly because he is apt to believe,
at the time, in most of the cases that he actually tries; and partly because he either abandons
or settles a large number of those he does not
believe in. But the lawyer recognizes that in
trying a case his prime duty is to present his
side to the tribunal fairly and as well as he
can, relying upon his adversary to present the
other side fairly and as well as he can. Since
the lawyers on the two sides are usually reasonably well matched, the judge or jury may ordinarily be trusted to make such a decision as
justice demands.

But when lawyers act upon the same principle in supporting the attempts of their private
clients to secure or to oppose legislation, a very
different condition is presented. In the first
place, the counsel selected to represent important private interests possesses usually
ability of a high order, while the public is often
inadequately represented or wholly unrepre-
sented. Great unfairness to the public is apt
to result from this fact. Many bills pass in

our legislatures which would not have become law, if the public interest had been fairly represented; and many good bills are defeated which if supported by able lawyers would have been enacted. Lawyers have, as a rule, failed to consider this distinction between practice in courts involving only private interests, and practice before the legislature or city council involving public interests. Some men of high professional standing have even endeavored to justify their course in advocating professionally legislation which in their character as citizens they would have voted against.

Furthermore, lawyers of high standing have often failed to apply in connection with professional work before the legislature or city council a rule of ethics which they would deem imperative in practice before the court. Lawyers who would indignantly retire from a court case in the justice of which they believed, if they had reason to think that a juror had been bribed or a witness had been suborned by their client, are content to serve their client by honest arguments before a legislative committee, although they have as great reason to believe that their client has bribed members of the legislature or corrupted public opinion. This confusion of ethical ideas is an important reason why the

Bar does not now hold the position which it formerly did as a brake upon democracy, and which I believe it must take again if the serious questions now before us are to be properly solved.

Here, consequently, is the great opportunity in the law. The next generation must witness a continuing and ever-increasing contest between those who have and those who have not. The industrial world is in a state of ferment. The ferment is in the main peaceful, and, to a considerable extent, silent; but there is felt to-day very widely the inconsistency in this condition of political democracy and industrial absolutism. The people are beginning to doubt whether in the long run democracy and absolutism can co-exist in the same community; beginning to doubt whether there is a justification for the great inequalities in the distribution of wealth, for the rapid creation of fortunes, more mysterious than the deeds of Aladdin's lamp. The people have begun to think; and they show evidences on all sides of a tendency to act. Those of you who have not had an opportunity of talking much with laboring men can hardly form a conception of the amount of thinking that they are doing. With many these problems are all-absorbing.

Many workingmen, otherwise uneducated, talk about the relation of employer and employee far more intelligently than most of the best educated men in the community. The labor question involves for them the whole of life, and they must in the course of a comparatively short time realize the power which lies in them. Often their leaders are men of signal ability, men who can hold their own in discussion or in action with the ablest and best-educated men in the community. The labor movement must necessarily progress. The people's thought will take shape in action; and it lies with us, with you to whom in part the future belongs, to say on what lines the action is to be expressed; whether it is to be expressed wisely and temperately, or wildly and intemperately; whether it is to be expressed on lines of evolution or on lines of revolution. Nothing can better fit you for taking part in the solution of these problems, than the study and preëminently the practice of law. Those of you who feel drawn to that profession may rest assured that you will find in it an opportunity for usefulness which is probably unequalled. There is a call upon the legal profession to do a great work for this country.